THE CONSTITUTIONAL CONVENTION, 1787

In 1787, fifty-five delegates from twelve of the thirteen American states gathered at the State House in Philadelphia, Pennsylvania, to revise the Articles of Confederation. (Rhode Island did not send representatives.) The delegates included many of the most learned men in the ten-year-old nation: George Washington, James Madison, Alexander Hamilton, George Mason, and Benjamin Franklin, to name but a few. For almost four months they discussed and debated to resolve the differences separating them. The result of their work was not amended Articles of Confederation but a new document, which has served ever since as the basic law of the United States of America—the Constitution.

PRINCIPALS

The fifty-five delegates to the Constitutional Convention of 1787.

A FOCUS BOOK

The Constitutional Convention, 1787

The Beginning of Federal Government in America

by Harold Cecil Vaughan

FRANKLIN WATTS
NEW YORK | LONDON | 1976

The author and publisher of the Focus Books
wish to acknowledge the helpful editorial
suggestions of Professor Richard B. Morris.

Cover design by Ginger Giles

Photographs courtesy of: Culver Pictures, Inc.: p.
8; The New York Public Library Picture Collection: pp. 12, 17, 22, 27, 47; Museum of Fine Arts,
Boston, M. & M. Karolik Collection: p. 34; National
Archives: pp. 42, 43, 71

Library of Congress Cataloging in Publication Data

Vaughan, Harold Cecil.
    The Constitutional Convention, 1787.

    (A Focus book)
    Bibliography: p.
    Includes index.
    SUMMARY: Describes the events leading up to
and during the Constitutional Convention and dis-
cusses its importance in subsequent American history.
    1. United States. Constitutional Convention,
1787—Juvenile literature. [1. United States. Constitutional Convention, 1787] I. Title.
JK146.V36   342'73'029   75-25726
ISBN 0-531-01104-6

Contents

Delegates to the
Constitutional Convention   1

Prelude   4

The Articles
of Confederation   7

The Confederation Fails   16

Organizing the Convention   24

The Convention
Goes to Work   52

The Ratification Struggle   74

Bibliography   81

Index   83

Dedicated to my niece
Meta Adele Brophy

The Constitutional
Convention, 1787

Delegates to the Constitutional Convention

Fifty-five men attended the Constitutional Convention of 1787 in Philadelphia. Nineteen other men received appointments to the convention but did not attend. Thirty-nine (the numbered names) signed the Constitution. For various reasons the other sixteen did not sign.

Eight of the delegates (A) signed the Declaration of Independence. Six of the delegates (B) signed the Articles of Confederation. Eight of the delegates (C) attended the First Continental Congress. The same eight and thirty-four other delegates (D) served in the Second Continental Congress and the Congress of the Confederation (1781–1787).

New Hampshire
1. John Langdon, 1741–1819 (D)
2. Nicholas Gilman, 1755–1814 (D)

Massachusetts
3. Nathaniel Gorham, 1738–1796 (D)
4. Rufus King, 1755–1827 (D)
   Elbridge Gerry, 1744–1814 (A) (B) (D)
   Caleb Strong, 1745–1819

Connecticut
5. William Samuel Johnson, 1727–1819 (D)
6. Roger Sherman, 1721–1793 (A) (B) (C) (D)
   Oliver Ellsworth, 1745–1807 (D)

New York
  7. Alexander Hamilton, 1755–1804 (D)
     Robert Yates, 1738–1801
     John Lansing, Jr., 1754–1829 (D)

New Jersey
  8. William Livingston, 1723–1790 (C) (D)
  9. David Brearley, 1745–1790
 10. William Paterson, 1745–1806
 11. Jonathan Dayton, 1760–1824
     William Churchill Houston, 1746–1788 (D)

Pennsylvania
 12. Benjamin Franklin, 1706–1790 (A) (D)
 13. Thomas Mifflin, 1744–1800 (C) (D)
 14. Robert Morris, 1734–1806 (A) (B) (C) (D)
 15. George Clymer, 1739–1813 (A) (D)
 16. Thomas Fitzsimons, 1741–1811 (D)
 17. Jared Ingersoll, 1749–1822 (D)
 18. James Wilson, 1742–1798 (A) (D)
 19. Gouverneur Morris, 1752–1816 (B) (D)

Delaware
 20. George Read, 1733–1798 (A) (C) (D)
 21. Gunning Bedford, Jr., 1747–1812 (D)
 22. John Dickinson, 1732–1808 (B) (C) (D)
 23. Richard Bassett, 1745–1815
 24. Jacob Broom, 1752–1810

Maryland
 25. James McHenry, 1753–1816 (D)
 26. Daniel of St. Thomas Jenifer, 1723–1790 (D)

27. Daniel Carroll, 1730–1796 (B) (D)
John Francis Mercer, 1759–1821 (D)
Luther Martin, 1748(?)–1826 (D)

Virginia

28. George Washington, 1732–1799
(*president of the Convention*) (C) (D)
29. John Blair, 1732–1800
30. James Madison, Jr., 1751–1836 (D)
Edmund Jennings Randolph, 1753–1813 (D)
George Mason, 1725–1792
George Wythe, 1726–1806 (A) (D)
James McClurg, 1746–1823

North Carolina

31. William Blount, 1749–1800 (D)
32. Richard Dobbs Spaight, 1758–1802 (D)
33. Hugh Williamson, 1735–1819 (D)
William Richardson Davie, 1756–1820
Alexander Martin, 1740–1807

South Carolina

34. John Rutledge, 1739–1800 (C) (D)
35. Charles Cotesworth Pinckney, 1746–1825
36. Charles Pinckney, 1757–1824 (D)
37. Pierce Butler, 1744–1822 (D)

Georgia

38. William Few, 1748–1828 (D)
39. Abraham Baldwin, 1754–1807 (D)
William Pierce, 1740–1789 (D)
William Houstoun, 1755–1813 (D)

Prelude

After years of what an ever-increasing number of American colonists felt to be intolerable actions on the part of the British government, discontent flared into revolution in 1775. The preceding year, in response to the Boston Tea Party—which had resulted in 342 chests of East India Company tea floating in Boston harbor—Parliament had passed, and King George III had signed, the Coercive, or Intolerable, Acts. Aimed at punishing the colony of Massachusetts, particularly the port of Boston, these measures aroused opposition toward Great Britain in the other colonies as well. With Virginia in the lead, all the colonies except Georgia appointed delegates to attend the First Continental Congress. The Congress met on September 5, 1774, in Philadelphia, the capital city of Pennsylvania and largest city in the American colonies.

In light of what would happen during the next ten years, this protest meeting proved to be far more significant than any of the men who attended could have imagined. The Congress was, in fact, the embryo of the first continental government in America.

The great majority of delegates were not yet thinking of total separation from Great Britain. Rather, they were demanding a clarification and reorganization of the relationship between the mother country and the colonies. Joseph Galloway of Pennsylvania proposed a solution. He thought the colonists should have their own Parliament—equal in power to Great Britain's. Each Parliament would have the power to veto the other's actions in regard to governing the American colonies. Galloway's plan for moderate reform was voted down. Instead, the Congress endorsed a Massachusetts plan, the Suffolk Resolves. Drafted by Joseph Warren, and accepted by the towns in the Boston area on September 9, 1774, the resolves proposed that the Coercive Acts be declared unconstitutional and void, that Massachusetts declare itself a free state, and that economic sanctions be instituted until the British government saw fit to repeal the objectionable legislation. Alternate proposals, such as those offered in pamphlets written by John Adams and Thomas Jefferson, were discussed, but no action was taken.

The chief action of the First Continental Congress was the adoption of a Declaration of Rights. It accused Parliament of unfair taxation, of burdening the colonies with having to support standing armies in times of peace, of disregarding petitions, and of passing unjust and cruel laws. The declaration also asserted the colonists' rights to life, liberty, and property, and "to a free and exclusive power of legislation in their several provincial legislatures . . . in all cases of taxation and internal polity [political organization]." Further, the Congress adopted an agreement called the Continental Association. It proposed a nonimportation, nonconsumption, and nonexportation boycott of Great Britain. The boycott would cut off imports completely after December 1, 1774, and exports after September 10, 1775, if by that time Parliament had not repealed the Coercive Acts. Congress adjourned on October 26 but decided to meet again on May 10, 1775, if by then Parliament had not acted to resolve the colonial grievances.

In England the British government continued to consider further steps. Attempts to get Parliament to recall the troops stationed in Boston or to repeal the Coercive Acts failed. Led by Prime Minister Lord North, the British decided to take an even firmer stand. On March 30, 1775, George III signed the New England Restraining Act, which prohibited the four New England colonies from trading anywhere in the world except with Great Britain and Ireland. They were also forbidden access to the vital fishing grounds off Newfoundland and Nova Scotia.

Even before word of this latest coercive measure reached America, British troops and colonial Minutemen clashed at Lexington and Concord. Still, the colonists hoped for compromise with the mother country. That hope was not dead when the Second Continental Congress met on May 10, 1775. Only after their appeals to King George III and Parliament proved useless did the delegates reluctantly take up the task of creating a new government to guide the infant American nation through its war for independence. Lacking any formal authorization by the thirteen states, the Congress simply exercised the powers of government that by common sense and general agreement seemed necessary to conduct the affairs of state and the waging of war.

The Articles
of Confederation

The delegates who gathered in Philadelphia in the spring of 1775 were confronted with a score of problems requiring immediate action. First came the question of what to do about the fighting in Massachusetts, and the even more recent seizure of the British forts at Ticonderoga and Crown Point in the New York colony by Benedict Arnold, Ethan Allen, and the Green Mountain Boys of Vermont. Congress decided to establish an "Army of the United Colonies for the defense of American liberty," and to incorporate in it the Massachusetts militia and other such groups. John Adams nominated George Washington as commander in chief, to head the Continental army. However, Washington did not take command of the forces besieging Britain's General Thomas Gage in Boston until July 2, by which time the Battle of Bunker Hill had already been fought.

The Congress also created a navy and authorized the sending of diplomatic agents to Europe. It approved a military campaign, under the command of Benedict Arnold, to march across Maine to Canada, where an attempt would be made to win that British colony to the cause of American freedom. Amazingly, all of these actions were presumably done in the name of George III! To explain this contradictory policy, the delegates called upon John Dickinson and Thomas Jefferson to draw up a Declaration on the Causes of Taking Up Arms. With questionable logic, the declaration argued that the American forces were not trying to break up the union with Great Britain. Rather, they were opposing the tyranny of bad counselors and ministers who had misled

*Black Minuteman Peter Salem
shooting British Major John Pitcairn
at the Battle of Bunker Hill*

the king. The firm resistance of the colonies, it was argued, would bring about the downfall of these bad counselors, lead to the repeal of their illegal and unjust acts, and restore the true and friendly relationship that ought to exist between George III and his distant subjects.

Such arguments were even endorsed by some of the opposition leaders in Britain. One of the most important of these was Lord Chatham, who upon hearing the news of Lexington and Concord declared, "I rejoice that America has resisted!" Fourteen months would pass before the realities of the situation destroyed all hope of reconciliation and the Continental Congress took the final step of declaring independence.

On June 7, 1776, Richard Henry Lee of Virginia introduced a resolution stating "that these United Colonies are, and of right ought to be, Independent States, that they are absolved from all allegiance to the British Crown, and that all political connection between them and the State of Great Britain is and ought to be totally dissolved." The resolution further proposed "that a plan of confederation be prepared and transmitted to the respective Colonies for consideration and approbation." A discussion on the motion followed, during which it was agreed that three committees should be established, although actual adoption of the motion itself did not come until July 2.

Under the leadership of Thomas Jefferson, the first committee was charged with drawing up a declaration that would state the reasons justifying independence. The second committee undertook the task of winning foreign allies. The third committee, headed by John Dickinson, drafted a confederation agreement. Out of the first came the Declaration of Independence, which the Congress formally adopted on July 4, 1776. From the second would eventually emerge two treaties with France. The efforts of Benjamin Franklin and his colleagues were rewarded in February, 1778, with a commercial agreement and the essential military alliance that pledged the power of the French monarchy to the cause of American independence. Out of the third came a new American government.

John Dickinson reported back to Congress in July, 1776, that his group had prepared a document entitled "Articles of Confederation and Perpetual Union." Although it was graciously received by the delegates, there was little rush to confirm by law the assumption of sovereign powers that the Second Continental Congress had seized and used. Moreover, colonies with small populations protested the provision of the Articles of Confederation that called for representation in the projected Congress to be based on numbers. At their demand several changes were made, the most important being that each new state would have a single vote in the new legislature. That done, the Congress adopted the Articles of Confederation on November 15, 1777, and passed the document on to the colonies for ratification.

Eleven of the colonies ratified quickly. Delaware hesitated for a time and then agreed, leaving Maryland the sole holdout. From February, 1779, to March 1, 1781, the new government remained stillborn until one final issue was solved. Maryland was concerned over the "western lands," that huge area stretching from the crest of the Appalachian Mountains to the banks of the Mississippi River. This land, still virgin forest occupied in most parts by Indians, was approximately half the land area of the original United States. Its value had long been recognized by land speculators and by the leaders of the seven coastal states who laid claim to it. Many of these claims conflicted. Virginia, for example, asserted its right to a vast area that ran as far west as the Mississippi River and as far north as the Great Lakes. This claim overlay territories that New York, Massachusetts, and Connecticut all claimed. Maryland, perhaps because it had no western land claim of its own, insisted that all the states give up their claims in favor of the new central government.

For a long time the seven states involved refused to act. Then New York agreed. Virginia followed on January 2, 1781. The other five states, none of whom was powerful enough to contest the issue with these two giants, did the same. With that battle won, Maryland ratified the Articles of Confederation on March 1, 1781.

Pealing church bells and a twenty-one-gun salute celebrated the birth of the new government. Samuel Huntington, last president of the Second Continental Congress, held a reception, and the official name of the body he headed now became the United States in Congress Assembled, sometimes called the Congress of the Confederation or simply "the Congress." The name change was actually only ceremonial. The same men continued to rule the nation during these last months before the final military victory at Yorktown. The great majority of Americans continued to refer to the governing body as the Continental Congress.

The Articles of Confederation were based, in part, on Benjamin Franklin's Albany Plan of Union, first proposed by him and Thomas Hutchinson in June, 1754. At that time conflicts between the mother country and the colonies led the two men to suggest that the crown appoint a colonial president. A grand council chosen by the colonial legislatures would aid the president. The plan was rejected. Franklin modified it and submitted it to the Continental Congress again in July, 1775. The

Farmers going off to fight.
They had little training and were
called Minutemen because
they pledged to be ready for
battle on a minute's notice.

modified plan called for representation in proportion to population and contributions from the colonies to a common treasury, but it stopped short of granting Congress the power to tax individuals. Dickinson and his committee used Franklin's ideas as a starting point in drawing up the Articles of Confederation.

In the articles, measures were taken to guarantee that no strong central government could develop and take power away from the states. Decisions on all important matters such as making war, ratifying treaties, borrowing money, or raising an army and navy required the assent of nine out of the thirteen states. And all the state legislatures had to agree to any changes in the articles. To maintain further the power of the states, the central government was given few means to enforce the limited powers it was granted. The central government could function only as long as it held the goodwill of the states. As an additional check on a strong central government, the judicial branch was given limited power. Finally, there was to be no chief executive, except for a president elected and controlled by the Congress.

On the important matter of congressional representation, Benjamin Franklin's advice was rejected. Each state was permitted one vote. Each was required to send no fewer than two and no more than seven members to the Congress, and no one of the delegates could serve more than three years over a six-year period.

Most of the power that the new Congress had was in the field of foreign affairs. Congress could deal with war and peace, conduct foreign relations, and settle disputes between the states, but it could not tax foreign or interstate commerce. Expenses required for the common defense or the general welfare were to be met by making requisitions on the states. The taxes to meet these requisitions, however, could be levied and collected only by the states.

Congress was given the power to create executive departments. It set up five of them, in the fields of finance, foreign affairs, war (army), marine (navy), and postal service. It could also set the value of coins, enact standards of weights and measures, establish post offices, and regulate "Indians, not members of any state."

In general, the new central government was permitted to exercise those powers which the states felt had once legitimately belonged to king and Parliament. Clearly the central government might advise, recommend, or request, but it could not force the states to act if they did not choose to do so.

This union of Great Britain's former colonies—under the Articles of Confederation—created a nation in which the central government was severely limited in its authority and could be almost totally paralyzed by action or inaction on the part of fewer than half of the states.

The Articles of Confederation represented the results of a conservative rather than a radical revolution. For all the restructuring of the form of government, there was little discussion of the extension of suffrage to those who did not have it, of whether or not the institution of slavery should be challenged, or if the economic system under which the nation was operating should be questioned. When on occasion such points were raised, they were ignored or disposed of as quickly as possible.

Radical change was not the goal of the delegates who had gathered in Philadelphia. These American leaders were mostly men of wealth, property, and social position. They were disputing what they considered the usurpation of power by king and Parliament. They did not intend any similar disputing of their own position in American society.

The war itself, however, did cause major changes. Disruption of trade with Great Britain and its colonies forced the finding of new markets. Speculation, profiteering, and inflation left their mark. So did the seizure of Loyalist (pro-British) property, the exodus of about eighty thousand persecuted supporters of the crown, and the disestablishment of the Anglican Church.

The Confederation Fails

From the time the Articles of Confederation went into effect in March, 1781, there were signs of weakness. Canada, a British colony, refused to join the Confederation. Vermont sought statehood, but was denied it because New York and New Hampshire, both of whom lay claim to Vermont's territory, blocked the request. Vermont would remain a territory with no voice in the central government until 1791. Statehood was also delayed for the proposed state of Franklin (later part of Tennessee) and Kentucky. The government's inability to act so annoyed the settlers in this region that by 1784 George Washington remarked that their very loyalty to the United States was in doubt. In spite of this and other warnings, Kentucky did not become a state until 1792 and Tennessee had to wait until 1796.

The feeble Congress of the Confederation could not even protect itself from assault. In 1783 a group of soldiers in Pennsylvania mutinied when their demands for long-overdue pay were ignored. Congress appealed to the state for protection. The request went unheeded, with the result that Congress had to flee for a time to Princeton College in New Jersey.

In the area of international affairs, too, Congress proved weak and ineffective. It could not, for example, enforce all the provisions of the treaty that formally ended the Revolutionary War. Congress had promised the other parties to the treaty that the states would return all Loyalist property taken during the war to the rightful owners. Except for Maryland and Pennsylvania, the states ignored this request. They also ignored the treaty provision for "no future confiscations." New York and

Tories, Americans loyal to Britain,
being chased out of town.
Many of them fled to Canada.
Their property in America
was seized and never returned.

South Carolina were the worst offenders. Congress had no power to force the states to comply with the terms of the treaty.

The question of prewar debts owed by Americans to British subjects created a similar problem. The peace treaty forbade any "legal impediment" being placed in the way of recovering debts. Virginia, the state whose citizens owed the most, argued that the debts had been canceled during the war by the state legislature and so no longer existed. Deadlock resulted, and the problem was not settled until 1802, thus having outlived the Articles of Confederation by almost fifteen years.

Congress was not only powerless to control the states but also powerless to protect the national interest when other countries threatened. At the end of the war the British held trading posts along the Canadian border at Ogdensburg, Oswego, Niagara, Detroit, and Michilimackinac. According to the treaty, they were to be given up as quickly as possible. Reluctant to stop the profitable trade with the Indians, the British government used the excuse that America's failure to honor other treaty provisions justified Britain's doing the same in this case. Not until war threatened to break out over this issue in 1796 did the British give up the posts, again many years after the demise of the articles.

United States relations with Spain in the South were hardly any better than with the British in Canada. Ignoring the terms of the peace treaty that concerned the Florida border, the Spanish encouraged the Indians to oppose new settlements of Americans in the southern parts of Alabama and Mississippi. Spain also refused for a time to allow the use of its port facilities at New Orleans. That single action threatened the economy of all the western lands whose settlers used the water network of the Ohio, Tennessee, and Mississippi rivers to trade with the rest of the world. Without the port, goods and supplies could not move to and from the riverboats to oceangoing vessels, and trading would cease. Except for sending a protest to the Spanish authorities and making an effort to negotiate the point, Congress was powerless.

In Europe there was more of the same. Too poor to pay blackmail as some other nations did, and too weak to fight, Congress watched in dismay as the Barbary pirates in the Mediterranean harassed and captured numerous American merchant ships and imprisoned hundreds of American seamen. Thomas Jefferson, then the United States minister to France, wrote, "We are the lowest and most obscure of the whole diplomatic tribe."

Financial troubles plagued Congress and the nation. During 1782–83 the Congress asked the states for contributions totaling $11 million. The states responded with less than half a million. Robert Morris, the superintendent of finance, made countless appeals to the states either to meet their assessments or to permit the Congress to levy taxes and establish a national tariff. When the states refused, he resigned.

More than half the states had attempted to meet their assessment by issuing vast amounts of paper money. The notes quickly went down in value, prices soared, and serious inflation resulted. The most extreme case was in Rhode Island. There the farmer-debtor group gained control of the legislature and passed a law requiring acceptance of the almost worthless paper money. Rather than take this currency, merchants closed their stores, hid their stock, or tried to export it to New York or the West Indies. The angry farmers then blockaded towns in an effort to starve the townspeople into submission. A civil war almost erupted.

Interstate tariff laws added another burden. Intended to protect local industry from out-of-state competition, as well as earn some additional revenue, these barriers soon led to tariff wars. New York levied a tax on foodstuffs coming from New Jersey and Connecticut and put a high entrance and clearance fee on all vessels coming from or bound for its neighboring states. Connecticut farmers fought back by boycotting New York markets, while New Jersey retaliated with a monthly tax of thirty pounds on a lighthouse New York had constructed on Jersey property at Sandy Hook. Congress looked on powerless to resolve the dispute. More and more Americans agreed with Washington that the Confederation was indeed "a half-starved limping government, always moving upon crutches and tottering at every step."

It would, of course, be possible to cite a number of achievements that took place during the seven years that the Articles of Confederation were the law of the land. The Congress did bring the war to a successful conclusion, and its representatives negotiated a favorable treaty of peace. Two excellent ordinances were enacted determining the future of the great Northwest Territory north of the Ohio River. Satisfactory trade treaties were signed with France, Sweden, the Netherlands, and a number of other nations. The beginning of the enormously profitable trade between New England and China began at this time. Taken as a whole, however, there were few observers who would have debated the general failure of the Confederation.

How many years the young government might have survived before total collapse is a historian's guessing game. That it was not permitted a slow and lingering death was due primarily to Shays' Rebellion. This uprising took place in western Massachusetts in 1786. At the time a conservative state government had chosen to ignore the plight of a vast number of poor farmers, many of them veterans of the Revolution who could no longer make ends meet. Mortgage foreclosures were at an all-time high and jails were overflowing with debtors. One such veteran farmer was Daniel Shays. During the Revolution he had fought bravely and had risen to the rank of captain. Now the owner of a debt-ridden farm, he joined his friends and neighbors in organizing protests against a government seemingly indifferent to their troubles. They demanded that the legislature immediately increase the supply of paper money in order to raise the market price of their produce, that it reduce their taxes, and that mortgage foreclosures be suspended. They also tried to frighten local judges into making decisions favorable to debtors who had been forced into court.

By the fall of 1786 these protesting farmers had succeeded in stopping courts from sitting in the four western counties of Massachusetts and at Concord in Middlesex County. The governor, James Bowdoin, a firm conservative, countered by issuing a ban on unlawful assemblies and by calling out the militia. The desperate farmers, led by a hesitant Shays, now serving as the chairman of a committee that hoped to block the sitting of the state supreme court at Springfield for fear it might indict them for treason, decided to act. Joining with other groups until they were more than a thousand strong, they moved against the courthouse and federal arsenal in Springfield on January 27, 1787. Loyal militia under the command of Major General William Shepherd drove them back after firing only one shot (the

*Massachusetts paper money
designed by Paul Revere.
Shortly after the notes appeared,
they became almost worthless,
and many ended up being used
as wallpaper in barbershops.*

militia alone was armed with artillery). Shortly after, an army led by General Benjamin Lincoln, and supported by contributions from a number of wealthy citizens, arrived to pursue the rebels. Several skirmishes followed. Shays's forces fell back to Petersham, where, after a confrontation on February 4, 1787, the revolt collapsed.

Although the rebellion had quickly fallen apart, businessmen, merchants, large landowners, and wealthy conservative elements throughout the country were deeply shocked. Fears of mob rule, chaos, and revolution stirred them as nothing else had done for the past six years. Suddenly demands were heard to strengthen the central government immediately so that it might serve as an effective weapon against these forces of lawlessness. From that point on, events moved swiftly, and the days of government under the Articles of Confederation were numbered.

Organizing the Convention

One of the many disputes between the states involved Virginia and Maryland. They argued over the control of the Potomac River boundary between them, and both claimed the area's rich oyster beds. In 1785 they met to discuss their differences, and a settlement was reached.

Pennsylvania and Delaware expressed interest in the settlement. Their ships and commerce passed up and down the Potomac. The Virginia legislature answered with a broad invitation to them and all the other states in the union to gather at Annapolis, Maryland, for a convention to be held in September, 1786, "to take into consideration the trade of the United States."

By the appointed date nine states had chosen delegates, but only those from Virginia, Delaware, Pennsylvania, New Jersey, and New York had arrived. Because of a misunderstanding in its own legislature, the host state of Maryland was not even represented. Among those who did appear was Alexander Hamilton from New York. Feeling that there was too little representation to accomplish any great change in the nation's commercial relations, he joined with James Madison and several others to prevent the conference from becoming a total failure. They got the delegates to accept a report drawn up by Hamilton. It contained a statement about the critical condition of the Confederation, and it then proposed that all thirteen states attend yet another convention that would "devise such further provisions as shall appear to them necessary to render the constitution of the federal government adequate to the exigencies of the Union."

Although the Continental Congress never formally acknowledged this call for a convention, it did eventually announce that there would be a general meeting of state delegations at the time and place suggested in Hamilton's report. Congress added, however, that the meeting would be for the sole purpose of revising the Articles of Confederation. In this manner the Constitutional Convention, as it later would be known, was convened in Philadelphia in May, 1787.

During the next seventeen weeks, until adjournment on September 17, fifty-five men would take part in the convention's deliberations. As a result of their efforts, the nation would be presented, not with suggested changes in the Articles of Confederation, but with a new blueprint for a strong federal union.

Twelve of the thirteen states sent delegations. The legislature of Rhode Island was deadlocked over the desirability of attending a convention in which it feared the conservatives and those in favor of a stronger central government would be the majority. As a result of the dispute, no delegates were appointed. From the other states, however, came individuals of such outstanding ability that Thomas Jefferson, then serving as minister to France and so unable to attend, referred to them as "an assembly of demigods." Although a big exaggeration when applied to some of the men present, by any objective standards the convention did contain an extraordinary number of brilliant scholars and statesmen. George Washington and Benjamin Franklin were already known abroad for their achievements. John Dickinson, Robert Morris, and more were by then well known throughout America. Most of the others were established leaders in their respective states.

Only two of the fifty-five delegates were similar to the typical American of the day—the independent, uneducated, small farmer of the back country. The delegates came almost entirely from homes close to the sea in the towns and villages or from great estates along the Atlantic coast. An occupational breakdown, hard to establish because so many of them were involved in more than one field, shows twenty-nine lawyers, thirteen planters or large-scale farmers, twelve state officeholders, eight merchants, and three physicians. At least a dozen were considered wealthy, while only nine were rated as of modest means or less. Every one at some point in his career had been on a public payroll. They had served as chief executives, administrators, and judges. Thirty had legislative experience. In an age when only a tiny fraction of the population received higher education, the convention boasted twenty-nine college graduates—ten from Princeton and two or more from such schools as William and Mary, Harvard, King's (now Columbia), and the College of Philadelphia (now the University of Pennsylvania). One delegate, Charles Cotesworth Pinckney of South Carolina, was a graduate of Oxford (England), and several others had studied in Europe.

The average age of the delegates was just over forty-three. Benjamin Franklin was the oldest at eighty-one. Five were under thirty; the youngest was twenty-six-year-old Jonathan Dayton of New Jersey. George Washington was fifty-five.

Most of those present were members of some Christian church: New England sent Congregationalists and Presbyterians; the South sent Episcopalians; and delegates from the Middle Colonies ranged from Quaker to Catholic. Only a handful, however, had any strong religious motivations. The great majority were highly rationalistic and secular in outlook.

Fifteen delegates owned enough slaves to earn money from their labor, and half a dozen others had black slave servants. Six

A view of the Philadelphia state house
as it looked in 1799. The original
caption to this picture described the
group of people in the foreground
as "a party of sightseeing Indians."

owned ships at sea. Ten invested in urban real estate, while twelve others held western lands for purposes of speculation.

Of overriding importance was the previous training these men had in the field of government on a national scale. Three had been in the Stamp Act Congress and eight in the First Continental Congress. Adding those in the Second Continental Congress (1775–1781) and the Congress of the Confederation (1781–1787) brings the total to forty-two. Eight had signed the Declaration of Independence, and six signed the Articles of Confederation. At least thirty had seen some military service during the Revolution.

For all the talent that was now about to undertake a huge task, it is unlikely that the convention or the new Constitution would have met with public approval had the key figure of George Washington been absent. At the war's end he had retired to his home at Mount Vernon determined to spend the rest of his years as a gentleman planter. He had refused to attend the Annapolis Convention in 1786 and at first declined to play any role in the newly proposed meeting. When Governor Edmund Randolph and James Madison pleaded with him to head the Virginia delegation, he cited the serious ill health of his mother and sister, his own rheumatism, and the demands of Mount Vernon as reasons for declining. Finally his fellow countrymen won him over by arguing that it was his duty to attend. On May 9 Washington left home for Philadelphia, where he would serve as presiding officer throughout the convention.

The first to arrive was James Madison, on May 3. Often called the "Father of the Constitution," this eager man approaching his thirty-sixth birthday had just left the Continental Congress in New York. There he had busied himself reading everything he could find on the subject of confederacies from the ancient Greeks to eighteenth-century Europe. He would prove to be the best prepared delegate and one of the most vocal. The record shows that this dedicated, forceful Virginian would address the convention 161 times, a record broken only by Pennsylvania's Gouverneur Morris and James Wilson.

Equally important in historical terms was Madison's record of the proceedings. Major William Jackson would become the official secretary of the convention, but he did little more than keep an account of motions and votes. Of his own accord, Madison took his seat in the front of the room directly in front of the president's desk, where he could clearly see and hear all that went on. Then, in his own system of shorthand, he took notes on the proceedings, later transcribing them into what is by far the best record of the convention. Half a dozen other delegates also took notes, but none supplied as much unbiased and accurate information as Madison.

On Sunday, May 13, cannons boomed as an honor guard greeted Washington on his arrival in Philadelphia. The city was then the largest in the country, with a population of 45,000 (only Boston, New York, Charleston, and Baltimore had populations larger than 10,000). One of Washington's first missions was a courtesy call on Benjamin Franklin, who as president of the Pennsylvania government was the host of the convention.

The next morning Washington appeared at the state house to find that only a handful of delegates had arrived. Pennsylvania's eight were present, probably because they all lived in Philadelphia. A majority of the Virginia delegates were also on hand, but that was all. It was agreed that no further action could be taken until a quorum—a majority—of seven states could be counted. This delayed the opening until Friday, May 25. Bad weather had slowed down some of those traveling from the more distant states, for transportation was an uncertain and risky business. Under the best of conditions, it could easily take two or three weeks for those coming from New Hampshire or Georgia to reach Philadelphia.

Not only did the convention need a quorum of seven states but a quorum within each state was also necessary. As a result there would be many occasions when even on the most important votes some states would be unable to cast a ballot. Specifically, the following requirements were laid down by the state legislatures as the quorum for their delegations:

Virginia	3 of 7	Georgia	2 of 4
New Jersey	3 of 5	New York	2 of 3
Pennsylvania	4 of 8	South Carolina	2 of 4
North Carolina	3 of 5	Massachusetts	3 of 4
New Hampshire	2 of 2	Connecticut	1 of 3
Delaware	3 of 5	Maryland	any of 5

For eleven days, therefore, no formal progress could be made. That did not prevent Madison from using the time to good advantage. In informal discussion at the Indian Queen, a coffee house and inn near the state house, he tried to get delegates to accept his view that the government needed immediate reform.

He found little cause for worry in the eight-man Pennsylvania delegation. Benjamin Franklin at eighty-one was ailing and could say little, but he was known to be a loyal supporter of Federalism—strong central government. His silent consent to the proceedings, along with his enormous prestige, carried great weight. George Clymer spoke on occasion but did not have much influence. Robert Morris, who was widely admired as the financial genius who almost singlehandedly had prevented the fall of the American government during the war, was also a Federalist, but he spoke only twice during the entire convention. Thomas Mifflin, who made only one contribution to the debate, and Thomas Fitzsimons, who never spoke at all, almost always supported Madison. So did Jared Ingersoll, who did not break his silence until the very last day of the convention. The remaining two Pennsylvanians more than made up for the silence of the others. Along with Madison, Gouverneur Morris and James Wilson were the most vocal men in the state house.

Gouverneur Morris, at thirty-five a fun-loving, high-living bachelor, was one of the chief surprises of the convention. A graduate of King's College (Columbia), he had practiced law successfully and, despite the loss of a leg in a carriage accident, was an active, forceful individual. (He was not related to Robert Morris.) He spoke on 173 occasions, more than any other delegate—all the more amazing since he was absent the last three weeks in June—and was highly praised for his frankness, insight, and superb timing. Madison later wrote that "to the brilliancy of his genius he added . . . a candid surrender of his opinions, when the lights of discussion satisfied him . . . and had a readiness to make the best of measures in which he had been overruled."

James Wilson, aged forty-five, who spoke on 168 occasions, was an equally successful lawyer. Although somewhat more serious than Morris in approach, he was no less zealous as he debated, drafted, and bargained for the Federalist ideas he so firmly believed in. Wilson had come to America from Scotland only twenty years earlier to teach school and had already won his place in American history as a signer of the Declaration of Independence and a longtime member of the Continental Congress.

Madison's own state of Virginia had elected a seven-man delegation. It matched that of Pennsylvania in the brilliance of its members but not in loyalty to Federalism. Fortunately, Madison could depend on the support of an important delegate from his state—George Washington. Beyond question the presence of George Washington meant more than that of any of the fifty-five men in assuring the ultimate acceptance of the convention's labors by the American people. The general willingness to permit secret deliberations would surely have been protested far more than it was if he had not been one of the delegates. As president of the convention he said little but never missed a single session, and on those occasions when he did enter the discussions he gave solid support to Madison.

George Wythe might have proven a powerful ally, but shortly after his arrival he was called home by the illness and subsequent death of his wife. He left Philadelphia on June 4 and never returned. James McClurg, one of the three physicians present, did the same in late July. He had been chosen to replace the anti-Federalist Patrick Henry, who had refused to attend the convention, remarking, "I smell a rat!" On only three occasions did McClurg speak, and then not to any great effect.

John Blair, although a Federalist, proved another disappointment. He never spoke or served on a committee. He did on occasion serve a purpose, however, for he held the swing vote. When Madison and Washington were opposed on some point by Randolph and Mason, it was Blair's vote that kept Virginia in the Federalist column.

Edmund Jennings Randolph, the governor of Virginia, proved to be little support for Madison. Son of a Loyalist who had fled the country in 1775, Randolph had chosen to follow the patriot cause. He was a graduate of William and Mary, had served on Washington's staff during the Revolution, and became the youngest delegate to the Virginia convention of 1776, where he helped to draft his state's constitution. For the next ten years he was attorney general of Virginia, in addition to doing double duty for two years as a member of the Second Continental Congress. In 1786, at the age of thirty-three, he was elected to succeed Patrick Henry as governor. In spite of this record he proved a lukewarm Federalist. Randolph opposed taking power away from the states. At the end, certain that the Constitution would not be ratified, he refused to sign it or even pledge himself to recommend it to his own state. Active in the debates, ambitious and powerful, he was one of the major opposition figures at the convention. Still later, during the struggle in Virginia, he switched sides once again and helped to win ratification.

George Mason, who arrived on May 16, the day after Randolph and McClurg, proved to be another leading anti-Federalist. The fifth most active speaker, who had his say on 136 occasions, he, too, refused to sign the completed Constitution. Mason, then sixty-two, was a planter aristocrat by birth and a republican by choice. His vast five-thousand-acre estate, not far from Mount Vernon, was worked by several hundred slaves, yet he continually spoke out against slavery and formulated a plan for freeing and resettling blacks in the western territories. In 1776 he had taken a leading role in drafting the Virginia state constitution. Included in it was the Declaration

Large cotton plantations worked
by black slaves spread throughout
the South during the 1700s and
1800s. When the abolition of slavery
was suggested at the Constitutional
Convention, many delegates argued
that the economic survival of the
South depended on slave labor.

of Rights guaranteeing freedom and equality to all men, which he had composed and from which Jefferson had drawn so heavily when he prepared the Declaration of Independence.

Mason suggested during the convention that such guarantees be included in the Constitution, but his proposal was turned down. This defeat was one of his chief reasons for refusing to support the Constitution.

On May 18 the third state delegation, or at least two of its three members—Robert Yates and Alexander Hamilton—appeared in Philadelphia from New York. Yates, a justice of the state supreme court, and the third New York delegate, John Lansing, Jr., the thirty-three-year-old mayor of Albany, who would arrive later, had been chosen with only one objective in mind. They were to oppose the efforts of Hamilton, who as a result was undoubtedly one of the most frustrated men at the convention. Although the very individual who had written the call for the Philadelphia meeting, Hamilton knew from the start that his own state's vote would, whenever cast, be against everything he hoped to achieve.

The cause of Hamilton's situation was Governor George Clinton. Long the most powerful figure in New York State politics, Clinton was a confirmed anti-Federalist. He had considered vetoing New York's participation in the convention, but had finally decided in favor of a delegation that would stand firm against any change in the Articles of Confederation. Hamilton hoped to have some of the state's other federally minded leaders, such as John Jay, appointed by the legislature, but Clinton proved strong enough to block that. This defeat, and the fact that Hamilton was the foremost advocate of a central government that would be stronger than any of the other delegates desired, may help to explain why he was one of the biggest disappointments at the convention. One might have expected Hamilton to equal or even surpass Madison as the chief architect of the new government, but this was not to be. Only for a short time in June, and then again in September, did he show the forceful talent and ability for which he was already justly famous.

Hamilton—brilliant, charming, ambitious, just thirty-two —brought to Philadelphia the experiences and learning of most men twice his age. An uncompromising nationalist, Hamilton knew from the beginning that neither his state nor the convention would agree with his answers to the nation's problems. Lansing and Yates cast New York's vote against him on every occasion until they tired of the game and left on July 10. Since they were necessary to make New York's quorum, their departure meant the state was no longer a voting member of the convention.

Next to put in an appearance, on May 21, were three members of the five-man delegation from Delaware. They were George Read; Richard Bassett, an ardent Methodist and possibly the most religious of all the delegates; and quiet Jacob Broom, a relatively unknown farmer who had earlier served in his state's legislature and had been appointed to the Annapolis Convention, which he chose not to attend. The three were a quorum. The other delegates, Gunning Bedford, Jr., and John Dickinson, soon joined them. The group proved to be strongly Federalist and except for the aging Dickinson had an excellent attendance record. However, only two of them played any significant role.

John Dickinson, like Benjamin Franklin, was a direct link

to the past. At fifty-five he was living in semiretirement when the call came. Then—as in 1765 when he left for the Stamp Act Congress, and in 1774 when elected to the First Continental Congress, and in 1775 when he returned to the Second Continental Congress—he marched off into the fray to do his legalistic conservative best. Dickinson was well known for two reasons: his presence at these important meetings and the fact that he wrote "Letters from a Farmer in Pennsylvania"—an examination of the problems that arise out of parliamentary control of colonies. In 1785 he moved to Dover, Delaware, and became a spokesman for a different state.

Dickinson had been chairman of the committee that drew up the Articles of Confederation. It is true that he refused to sign the Declaration of Independence, and that while a power in Pennsylvania politics he had been an enemy of Benjamin Franklin's and a leading anti-Constitutionalist. But now he was less certain of the evils of a stronger central government. He endorsed the idea of a federal union and then spent most of his time seeing that his recently adopted state would not be swallowed up by its giant neighbors, Pennsylvania and Virginia. He did his job well, then fled back to his home on September 14, asking George Read to sign his name when the embossed copy of the Constitution was ready.

Read was the other outstanding Delaware representative. A lawyer and veteran of the Revolution, he, too, attended both Continental Congresses. He voted against independence, but when the motion carried he signed the declaration. Now he battled alongside Dickinson to maintain the principle of state equality within the stronger union he had come to desire.

North Carolina's representatives joined the growing assembly on May 22. The state's delegation was divided into several factions. Alexander Martin, who like so many others combined his role as a plantation owner with the law, quickly joined the anti-Federalist forces. A veteran who had been accused of cowardice during the Battle of Germantown, he was nevertheless popular in North Carolina, where he had been elected to serve four years in the senate, two on the board of war, and three as governor. He left the convention in disgust late in August, not having made a single contribution to the discussions.

The second delegate who refused to sign was William Richardson Davie. Like Martin, he was a Princeton graduate and left the convention early, returning to North Carolina on August 13. There, however, the similarity ended, for Davie departed because of boredom with, rather than opposition to, the growing success of the Federalists. To the extent that he took part, Davie might be described as a moderate Federalist, and he did major service in helping to settle the dispute between the large and small states.

The senior member from North Carolina was Hugh Williamson. This well-educated physician, who at fifty-two could recall having witnessed the Boston Tea Party and having carried news of the event across the Atlantic to Benjamin Franklin in London, was the most devoted Federalist. He would serve on five committees, take an active part in the debates, and prove to be of enormous value to his side.

Then there was Richard Dobbs Spaight, a twenty-nine-year-old, well-to-do planter. He tended to straddle controversial issues and to look to others for leadership and direction. He made a few minor contributions.

William Blount, on the other hand, arrived long after his colleagues, on June 20, and left on July 1 to return to New York, apparently preferring to continue his work in the Continental Congress. He did return, but not until August 7. Having considerable interest in land settlement and speculation in the Tennessee area, he might have been the convention's spokesman for Americans who had migrated west, but was not. Instead, like Jared Ingersoll of Pennsylvania, he never served on a committee and spoke for the first time on the very last day of the convention.

South Carolina was the next state to be represented. Its four-man delegation would constitute one of the most unified and homogeneous of the twelve delegations present in Philadelphia. All of the South Carolinians were prominent planter aristocrats and dedicated, if moderate, Federalists. Although their state was small, their pride rivaled that of the Virginians, and they were determined not to accept second place to any other group.

Dean of the South Carolina delegation was John Rutledge, one of the South's most devoted patriots. Just as he had worked furiously in the cause of American freedom long before the Revolution by opposing the tyranny of king and Parliament, he now labored to help produce the best possible government. Five of the convention's committees counted him as a member, and he was active on each. In the past, he had also served as his state's first governor and had proven a strong leader when, in the latter part of the Revolution, the war raged in the South. He had also seen service in the Continental Congress.

Supporting Rutledge were the two Pinckneys, General Charles Cotesworth and his second cousin Charles. The general had spent much of his youth in England, studying at Oxford and learning law from Blackstone. He was probably the best-educated delegate at the convention; however, his good reputation was based even more on his excellent war record. He had helped to fight off a British invasion of South Carolina in 1776, served as an aide to Washington at the battles of Germantown and Brandywine Creek, and even survived capture by the enemy in 1780. Both he and Rutledge were such well-known rebels that their estates were confiscated. By 1787, however, they had been able to rebuild their fortunes successfully.

Charles Pinckney, at twenty-nine, was a dozen years younger than his famous cousin, but by no means lived under his shadow. Charles, too, had fought in the war and been captured by the British, who had seized his property. Now he was a hardworking lawyer and planter and had just completed three years as one of the most active members in the Continental Congress. There he favored change aimed at strengthening the government under the Articles of Confederation.

For all his achievements, Charles Pinckney was not above claiming to be twenty-four years old in order to win the added distinction of being the youngest delegate at the convention. (Jonathan Dayton, twenty-six, of New Jersey was the youngest.) Pinckney never did win the acclaim he sought so aggressively. And his constant striving for recognition caused a number of those he worked with to give him the nickname "Me-too Charlie."

Pierce Butler, the son of an Anglo-Irish member of Parliament, was named as the fourth South Carolina delegate. Both Rutledge and General Pinckney had younger brothers of sufficient stature to be appointed to the post. Neither got the job for fear that powerful men in the state and voters might be upset if only two families controlled the convention delegation. Butler had first seen America when he landed in Boston as a commissioned officer in a British army regiment. He resigned in 1773, married an heiress, and settled in South Carolina, where he soon became a successful planter and an enthusiastic American patriot. Butler proved to be a statesman who could never give unquestioned support to either the states' rights advocates or the Federalists. He approached the idea of a strong central government with caution, seeking as many safeguards as possible to protect the states from becoming powerless.

Eleven days had now passed since the convention was scheduled to begin, and so far only six states had a quorum. Finally, on May 25, the New Jersey contingent arrived. It was made up of David Brearley, William Paterson, and William Churchill Houston. These three men were part of a seven-man commission that the Jersey legislature, first in the nation to act, had chosen to speak for their state. The group proved to be something of a disappointment. Two members, Abraham Clark and John Nielson, never bothered to appear in Philadelphia. Another, William Churchill Houston, became ill after one week, returned to Princeton, where he was a professor of mathematics, and died soon after. William Livingston, the governor of New Jersey, was so busy with state matters that he did not appear until June 5. Whenever present he put his considerable talents to use, but he was absent again from July 3 to 19 and on several other occasions. The youngest delegate to the convention, Jonathan Dayton, also arrived late and was frequently absent. But he proved one of the outstanding men at the convention. His performance in Philadelphia added to his already remark-

The most influential delegates
to the Constitutional Convention

Key for identification:

1. Edmund Jennings Randolph, Virginia
2. Nathaniel Gorham, Massachusetts
3. John Dickinson, Delaware
4. John Rutledge, South Carolina
5. James Wilson, Pennsylvania
6. Oliver Ellsworth, Connecticut
7. Charles Pinckney, South Carolina

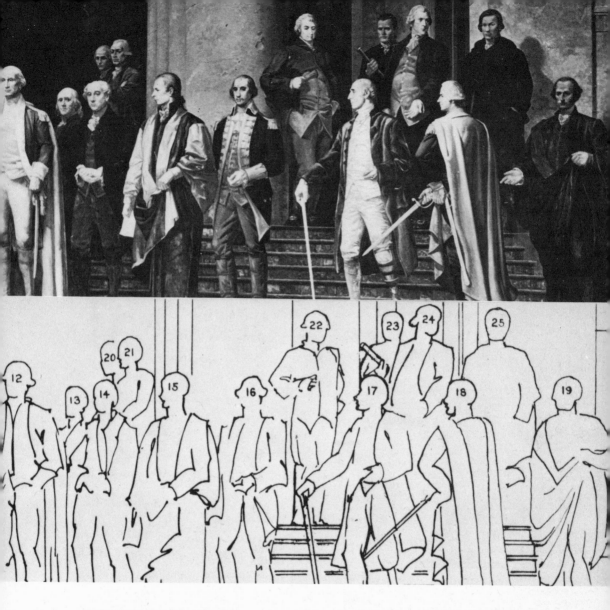

8. James Madison, Jr., Virginia
9. Elbridge Gerry, Massachusetts
10. William Samuel Johnson, Connecticut
11. George Mason, Virginia
12. George Washington, Virginia
13. Benjamin Franklin, Pennsylvania
14. Rufus King, Massachusetts
15. William Paterson, New Jersey
16. Charles Cotesworth Pinckney, South Carolina

17. Gouverneur Morris, Pennsylvania
18. Alexander Hamilton, New York
19. George Read, Delaware
20. William Richardson Davie, North Carolina
21. John Langdon, New Hampshire
22. Luther Martin, Maryland
23. Roger Sherman, Connecticut
24. Gunning Bedford, Jr., Delaware
25. Abraham Baldwin, Georgia

able record, which included a degree from Princeton, the rank of captain during the Revolution, survival as a prisoner-of-war, and a budding career in law and politics in New Jersey.

The last two Jersey men were the most effective. William Paterson, who had been brought to America at the age of two from Ireland, became one of his state's most promising politicians and lawyers. By 1779 he had become the attorney general of New Jersey. Four years later he decided to leave the political arena and devote himself to private law practice. When the call came, however, he agreed to serve. During the months in Philadelphia he became the chief spokesman for those who defended the rights of the small states. Supporting him in this was his friend and associate, the quiet, modest David Brearley, chief justice of the New Jersey supreme court. As chairman of the committee on postponed matters, Brearley proved a hardworking individual whose contribution, if not as dramatic as some, was essential to the success of the evolving Constitution.

At long last, by May 25, the convention had the necessary seven states, each with a quorum. As for the remaining five states, their delegations were yet to be seen, save for two individuals. William Few, one of the poorest members, had preceded the other three men who would represent Georgia. Few was born on a Maryland farm and worked as a bricklayer and farmer in North Carolina before moving to Georgia. He consistently neglected his personal affairs through the years to serve his state in a score of offices. Elected to the Continental Congress in 1780 and again in 1786 by his devoted neighbors, he had always done a good job and would do so again in the months ahead.

The other lone delegate, Rufus King of Massachusetts, was the first and only New Englander to have appeared up to that point. This disturbed both King and those who were anxious that the convention truly represent every section of the nation. King was another of the up-and-coming young men to attend. Just turned thirty-two, he had spent the war years studying at Harvard, soldiering part-time in Rhode Island, and reading law as well. In 1784 he went to New York, having been elected to the Continental Congress, and it was there that his ability began to show. In the years immediately preceding the convention he had been a supporter of anti-Federalists such as John Hancock and his soon-to-arrive colleague Elbridge Gerry. Shays' Rebellion had shaken King's belief in state supremacy, however, and when he reached Philadelphia, Alexander Hamilton appears to have won him over to unqualified support for a strong central government. Despite the quickness of the conversion, King proved to be one of Federalism's most loyal and outspoken champions.

By May 28, a Monday morning, several more delegates were on hand. The ailing Franklin had recovered enough to appear, along with Mifflin, Clymer, and Ingersoll, all of whom missed the first meeting in spite of the fact that they were from the host state. The only delegate from New England, Rufus King, also felt better, for Nathaniel Gorham and Caleb Strong now showed up, giving Massachusetts the three-man quorum needed for voting. Gorham had only recently completed a term as president of the Congress under the Articles of Confederation and so added prestige to both his state delegation and the convention itself. Still, neither he nor Strong nor King nor Judge Francis Dana, who because of sickness and the pressure of judical business never honored his appointment by appearing in Philadelphia, would prove as important as the fourth delegate, who arrived the next morning.

One might guess that the fourth delegate would be one of Massachusetts's three most famous sons, but such was not the case. John Adams was busy abroad, trying to represent his country in England. John Hancock had just been elected governor of his state and was about to enjoy again the office he had held five times. Sam Adams, aging and uncertain of his views about changing the government, decided against going. In his place, therefore, went his friend Elbridge Gerry. A lean and active Harvard man, Gerry had a good reputation throughout Massachusetts and the nation as a politician and statesman. He had signed both the Declaration of Independence and the Articles of Confederation. Known as a rock-ribbed Republican, he was so opposed to standing armies that he wanted to abolish the veterans' organization called the Order of the Cincinnati. And although an anti-Federalist in general, on many occasions he took the Federalist side. The largest holder of continental securities at the convention, Gerry had invested heavily in western lands and was disturbed by the declining economy of his hometown port of Marblehead, all of which made him see the value of a stronger central government. So had Shays' Rebellion, which frightened all men of property, making them wonder if any state government could stand alone against a hostile organized "rabble." Everyone knew that Gerry would have much to say before deliberations ended, although on which side no one could be sure.

Other new faces that Monday morning included the attorney general of Delaware, Gunning Bedford, Jr. Obese and outspoken, he enthusiastically defended small states like his own. James McHenry of Maryland, a likable Irish-born gentleman of thirty-four, was not widely known. Oliver Ellsworth, the first Connecticut delegate, was another of the nine Princeton

*Militiamen fire on rebels
during Shays' Rebellion.*

graduates at the convention. Ellsworth, like many of his colleagues, had tried schoolteaching and theology before deciding on law and public service. Financial success followed, and in 1785 he became a judge on the superior court of Connecticut. A tall man, well known for talking to himself and for his excessive use of snuff, Ellsworth was one of the top half-dozen men at the convention, contributing greatly to the solution of some difficult problems.

Ellsworth's first contribution was to announce the fact that his two colleagues would arrive shortly. One would be Dr. William Samuel Johnson of Stratford—an aristocrat from New England. As Johnson rode south to Philadelphia, he received word that he had been appointed president of Columbia College. The school, formerly King's College, had been reopened at the end of the Revolution and renamed Columbia. Johnson had won his bachelor's degree at Yale and his master's at Harvard. In spite of his conservative outlook, he attended the Stamp Act Congress in 1765, and during the following four years he represented Connecticut as its agent in London. While abroad, he won a doctorate from Oxford and made good friends of Benjamin Franklin and Dr. Samuel Johnson. Although he would speak less than either of his colleagues, this kind and gentle man played an important role and was especially influential on the Committee of Style.

The contributions of Roger Sherman had to be substantial indeed if he were to be rated higher than the other two voices from Connecticut. Most historians agree he made the grade. Although pious, honest, and serious, he was so ungainly that there was almost something comical about him. A jack-of-all-trades, he had tried everything from farming and cobbling to surveying and shopkeeping. He published almanacs, taught himself law, and often occupied several public offices at the same time. Yale gave him an honorary degree for his excellent service as college treasurer and bookstore owner. He was elected to both Continental Congresses and served on the committee that drafted the Declaration of Independence, which he signed. At the same time, he served on the committee that wrote the Articles of Confederation. All the while he somehow managed to support a large family. At the convention he ranked with Few and Pierce of Georgia as one of the three poorest delegates. Although the Connecticut delegation was smaller than those from most states, it was second to none in quality. The delegation would take its stand in the center, as Sherman's mild pro-state leanings balanced the similar moderately pro-Federal ideals of Ellsworth and Johnson.

May 30 was the occasion for the first appearance of William Pierce. Georgia was to be represented by a six-man delegation that would prove the least distinguished of any state. Two of those chosen never appeared in Philadelphia. William Few, who preceded Pierce; William Houstoun, who followed him by twenty-four hours; and Abraham Baldwin, who checked in ten days later, contributed little of importance to the debates, although they generally cast Georgia's vote in favor of a stronger federal union.

In most respects Pierce resembled his colleagues, save for the fact that he kept a journal. Unlike Madison, whose notes dealt with the substance of the discussions, Pierce wrote sketches of the delegates, commenting on each man's age, appearance, and oratorical abilities. Relatively little is known about him except for his excellent war record and that he had once been a prosperous import-export merchant. By the time of the Convention, however, he was on the verge of financial disaster.

He had definite opinions about those he observed during the next few weeks. In general he was impressed by their quality, although few measured up to his taste for flowery speaking. At the end of June he packed his bags and left for New York City, where Congress was sitting, apparently preferring his seat in the Congress to one at the convention.

One of the leading spokesmen for the smaller states, Luther Martin of Maryland, took his seat for the first time on Saturday, June 9. Already present from Maryland was Daniel of St. Thomas Jenifer, a sixty-four-year-old wealthy planter and friend of George Washington. So, too, was James McHenry, an Irish-born physician who by thirty-four had already retired from practice in order to live a gentleman's life on the fortune he had inherited from his father. McHenry had served with Hamilton as one of Washington's aides during the Revolution. Appearing on May 28, he stayed four days before leaving to visit his sick brother in Maryland. He did not return until August 6. The fourth Maryland delegate, Daniel Carroll, had reservations about spending a hot and uncomfortable summer in Philadelphia. After a late arrival on July 9, he settled down and led Daniel of St. Thomas Jenifer and McHenry in support of moderate Federalism. The remaining Maryland delegate, twenty-eight-year-old John Francis Mercer, sided with Luther Martin against the other three. Mercer attended the convention only from August 6 to 17, and during that time he was loud and ill-tempered and let everyone know he didn't like what was going on.

Although totally opposed to Alexander Hamilton's views on the shape of the new government, Luther Martin shared with him the frustration of being part of a delegation that always voted against everything he believed in. Yet Martin, too, would prove to be a major influence on the deliberations. Approaching forty, he was brilliant, hardworking, heavy-drinking, ornery, and the attorney general of Maryland. The son of a poor New Jersey farmer, he had saved enough money to attend Princeton and graduate with honors. He taught school in Maryland before becoming a lawyer. After distinguished service in the Revolution, he took great pleasure in prosecuting Loyalists and giving them harsh punishments. He also made a great deal of money, but spent it lavishly and so never became wealthy. Elected to the Continental Congress in 1784, Martin soon made clear that his primary loyalty was to his state, a position he would consistently maintain in Philadelphia until he left the convention in disgust on September 4.

Of the New Hampshire delegation, only John Langdon and Nicholas Gilman, two of the four men chosen to represent that state, ever arrived. This northernmost of all the states was not anxious to help strengthen the union and so failed to offer financial aid to those who were asked to make the long, tedious journey to Philadelphia. Langdon, a wealthy Portsmouth merchant, grew to favor a stronger central government once he realized its value in the field of international and interstate trade and commerce. As a result, he paid the cost of the delegation out of his own pocket, and on two dozen occasions he spoke up for the cause of moderate nationalism. Gilman, the choice of General John Sullivan—the most powerful man in the state, who might have come himself but for the fact that he was then serving as the president of New Hampshire—generally followed Langdon's lead, although there is no record of his ever having taken part in the proceedings.

The Convention
Goes to Work

Friday, May 25, 1787, was an unpleasant, rainy day. After the delegates gathered and it was determined that voting quorums from seven states were present, the first meeting of the Constitutional Convention got under way.

Pennsylvania's Robert Morris rose to speak for the ailing and absent Benjamin Franklin. He read a statement nominating George Washington as chairman, or president, of the convention. John Rutledge, next to Franklin in seniority, seconded the motion, which was carried unanimously. Then the most outstanding of all Americans was escorted to the chair on a dais behind the desk on which the Declaration of Independence had been signed. Washington gave a short acceptance speech, noting his inexperience in such a role, and pleaded in his sincere and modest fashion for forgiveness of such errors as he might make.

Aside from the appointment of a committee composed of Wythe, Hamilton, and Charles Pinckney, which was directed to draw up the rules of procedure for future meetings, little else was done. The delegates parted for the weekend. Washington and some of the others spent part of the weekend attending a service at the nearby Roman Catholic church. Many states did not allow open Catholic worship. The service was a "first" for many, including Washington.

Little happened on the second day of the convention, Monday, May 28, except to hear the report from the committee on rules and to vote unanimously that seven states (out of a possible twelve, since Rhode Island still remained firm in refusing to take part) would make a quorum. In addition, the delegates agreed to rules of secrecy. They decided to exclude the press, and each delegate pledged not to disclose anything about the deliberations. The delegates reasoned that this would help everyone to feel free to express his ideas. Secondly, North Carolina's Spaight recommended a rule that would permit review and revision of all resolutions passed if the membership so desired. By that time it was close to four in the afternoon, so work was halted until eleven the next morning, these being the hours established for the daily meetings.

It was on the third day, May 29, that the important work of the convention really began. Suggestions on reconsideration of resolutions and press attendance were discussed, strengthened, formalized, and passed. In the first case, it was decided that resolutions passed might be taken up again on the same day if unanimous consent were given; otherwise, after a day's notice in advance with only majority consent. As for Pierce Butler's resolution on secrecy, not only were the press barred and the delegates pledged not to leak any information, but it was agreed that the publication of any journal or notes about the convention would be forbidden.

Governor Edmund Randolph then rose to present the fifteen articles that would henceforth be known as the Virginia Plan and that would in essence represent the kind of government favored by the largest and most powerful of the states. He began by praising the Articles of Confederation—four of their framers (Gerry, Dickinson, and the two Morrises) were listening to his remarks. Then he pointed out that the articles had been adopted during a war emergency and were no longer adequate. The delegates were told that the plan he would now submit was not complete, not the final word. It was meant to serve as a basis on which discussion might begin.

On the morning of May 30, the discussion began. But not before the convention had devised a plan that would censor the information included in the record of the deliberations. The convention first voted to sit as a committee of the whole. This meant that the delegates had voted themselves into a committee composed of all the members. Having done so, they could then examine the issues informally without any records being kept. Once some sort of agreement had been reached, the committee of the whole would then dissolve itself and meet once again as the official convention ready officially to receive and note such information as the committee (in fact, the convention delegates) might choose to bring before it. Certainly, interesting and provocative details of so-called informal discussion were never recorded. Votes were taken only when the delegates met as the official convention.

The meeting began at ten o'clock (the eleven o'clock opening having been advanced so that more work could be done before adjournment at four). There was an immediate vote to form the committee of the whole. Washington stepped down, as he would do so often, and joined the Virginia delegation. Judge Nathaniel Gorham of Massachusetts took his place as chairman of the committee of the whole and conducted the meeting until a few minutes before four. Then the committee voted itself back into session as the convention and Washington returned to his seat on the dais. Such practice became standard operating procedure almost daily during the next few months.

The Virginia Plan not only called for the creation of a far stronger central government but saw to it that, when established, the central government would be dominated by those states with the largest population and the greatest wealth. Briefly, the fifteen points were:

1. *Resolved*, That the articles of Confederation ought to be so corrected and enlarged as to accomplish the objects proposed by their institution; namely, common defense, security of liberty, and general welfare.

2. *Resolved*, therefore, That the rights of suffrage, in the National Legislature ought to be proportioned to the quotas of contribution, or to the number of free inhabitants, as the one or the other rule may seem best in different cases.

3. *Resolved*, That the National Legislature ought to consist of two branches.

4. *Resolved*, That the members of the first branch of the National Legislature ought to be elected by the people of the several States. . . .

5. *Resolved*, That the members of the second branch of the National Legislature ought to be elected by those of the first, out of a proper number of persons nominated by the individual Legislatures. . . .

6. *Resolved*, That each branch ought to possess the right of originating Acts; that the National Legislature ought to be impowered to enjoy the Legislative Rights vested in Congress by the Confederation, and moreover to legislate in all cases to which the separate States are incompetent, or in which the harmony of the United States may be interrupted by the exercise of individual Legislation; to negative all laws passed by the several States, contravening in the opinion of the National Legislature the articles of Union; and to call forth the force of the Union against any member of the Union failing to fulfil its duty under the articles thereof.

7. *Resolved*, That a national executive be instituted; to be chosen by the National Legislature . . . and that besides a general authority to execute the National Laws, it ought to enjoy the Executive rights vested in Congress by the Confederation.

8. *Resolved*, That the executive and a convenient number of the National Judiciary, ought to compose a council of revision with authority to examine every act of the National Legislature before it shall operate, and every act of a particular Legislature before a Negative thereon shall be final. . . .

9. *Resolved*, That a national judiciary be established to consist of one or more supreme tribunals and of inferior tribunals to be chosen by the National Legislature . . . to hear and determine in the first instance, and of the supreme tribunal to hear and determine, in the dernier resort, all piracies and felonies on the high seas; captures from an enemy; cases in which foreigners or citizens of other States applying to such jurisdictions may be interested, or which respect the collection of the National revenue; impeachments of any National officer; and questions which involve the national peace or harmony.

10. *Resolved*, That provision ought to be made for the admission of States lawfully arising within the limits of the United States, whether from a voluntary junction of Government and Territory, or otherwise, with the consent of a number of voices in the National Legislature less than the whole.

11. *Resolved*, That a Republican Government and the territory of each State . . . be guaranteed by the United States to each State.

12. *Resolved*, That provision ought to be made for the continuance of Congress and their authorities and privileges, until a given day after the reform of the articles of Union shall be adopted. . . .

13. *Resolved,* That provision ought to be made for the amendment of the articles of Union whensoever it shall seem necessary; and that the assent of the National Legislature ought not be required thereto.

14. *Resolved,* That the legislative, executive, and judiciary powers within the several States, ought to be bound by oath to support the articles of union.

15. *Resolved,* That the amendments which shall be offered to the Confederation by the Convention ought at a proper time, or times, after the approbation of Congress, to be submitted to an assembly or assemblies of Representatives, recommended by the several Legislatures to be expressly chosen by the people, to consider and decide thereon.

At Randolph's clever suggestion, the third point—concerning a two-branch legislature—was discussed first. His strategy was aimed at winning a crucial victory on the first test of Federalist strength. What Randolph and his allies hoped to gain was approval of a major change in the Articles of Confederation: That is, a change so great as to make it clear that the articles were actually being replaced rather than amended. Consent to point three would accomplish that very end, with the added advantage of dealing with a specific and popular change. Only Benjamin Franklin and Roger Sherman preferred a unicameral, or one-house legislature, and neither cared enough to do more than offer token resistance. Had the discussion started on the first point, which was extremely general in scope, no clear-cut decision would likely have resulted. To have begun on point two meant dealing with the suffrage question, one of the most difficult problems facing the delegates, and would probably have shattered the convention beyond repair.

Discussion on point three was decidedly in favor of a bicameral congress. Gouverneur Morris, in particular, gave a spirited speech, warning that if this vital change was not made and the existing weak government continued, the nation would pass into the hands of a despot—ruler with absolute power and authority—within twenty years.

When the vote came, New York was unable to cast a ballot since Yates and Hamilton were on opposite sides; neither could New Jersey, which that day lacked a quorum. Sherman cast Connecticut's vote in the negative. The aye votes came from Delaware, Virginia, the two Carolinas, Pennsylvania, and Massachusetts. The die was cast. The American nation would be offered a constitution rather than an improved version of the Articles of Confederation.

The delegates now turned to point four of the Virginia Plan. Gerry and Sherman criticized the idea that the first branch of the national legislature should be popularly elected. They said that the ordinary American was ill informed and subject to listening to dishonest candidates who promise anything in order to get elected. The people, said Gerry and Sherman, could not make intelligent decisions. Mason and Wilson defended the will of the people as "the grand depository of the democratic principles of the Government." When the vote came, the point was carried six to two for popular elections, with two states split. A major decision had been made; however, it was not yet a final victory. The opponents of a popularly elected house would challenge it again in future meetings.

The May 30 session also produced a unanimous vote in favor of allowing both houses of the national legislature to propose new laws. The day had been most productive.

On the first day of June the convention turned its attention to one of the most important sections of Randolph's proposals, point seven, the question of a national executive authority. A score of delegates rose to present a variety of viewpoints. Wilson, Rutledge, and Charles Pinckney all favored a single executive. Fearing that this smacked of kingship, Randolph called for an executive with three men. Mason agreed but suggested that each man represent one of the three geographic sections of the country. Madison was more concerned with the powers to be granted to the executive branch than with how many office holders it had. Wilson advocated a three-year term of office with reelection or reappointment possible. Charles Pinckney argued in favor of a single seven-year term, and just before adjournment this proposal carried by a five-to-four vote, with Massachusetts divided. Later on, this decision would be changed with final acceptance of a single executive to serve a four-year term with the possibility of being reelected.

For the first thirteen days of June discussions of the various points in the Virginia Plan continued. More and more of the delegates spoke out as issues of personal concern were raised, or as some point was discussed that directly related to their particular state or section. Some suggestions, such as Franklin's proposal that the national executive serve without pay, were examined at great length and then turned down. Other proposals, like Wilson's idea that the executive be chosen by a group of so-called electors elected themselves by the people in agreed-upon districts, were first rejected and then later changed and incorporated into the final document—this one as the electoral college. On rare occasions a motion won unanimous consent, as on the vote to give the executive authority an absolute veto over legislative acts. However, after Gerry protested this power as being extreme, it was changed to allow the legislature to override the executive veto by a two-thirds vote in each house of the Congress.

At times the delegates were so uncertain of what they wanted that they changed their decisions on the same day. On June 5 they voted in favor of a national judiciary "to consist of one supreme tribunal and of one or more inferior tribunals." Governor Livingston of New Jersey, who had only arrived that morning, objected, whereupon the convention voted to strike out "one or more inferior tribunals," thus switching to a single rather than a multiple court system. Hours later, when Madison proposed that the legislature not be given the power to appoint national judges, his motion carried nine to two.

As the discussion of the Virginia Plan progressed, several prime concerns became increasingly obvious. With few exceptions, such as Hamilton and Read, the great majority of all those present agreed that while the powers of the new central government should be strengthened, such changes should not destroy the existence of the individual states or render them totally powerless. The delegates were completely opposed to creating a government similar to that of Great Britain. Although the delegates could see the great value to be gained from a tighter union of the thirteen almost totally independent states, they were suspicious and fearful of a centralized national state. This deeply rooted concern was also responsible for the generally accepted practice of separating the limited powers given to the national government among its three branches—the legislative, executive, and judicial. The representatives were making every effort to prevent the rise of a dictatorial president, legislative body, or court. That they succeeded is seen clearly in the division of powers between the states and the national, or federal, government, and the separation of powers among the three branches of that federal government.

Another main concern was the conflict between the big states and the small. Some might have predicted with considerable logic that the main division would have been caused by geography. Certainly there were great sectional differences between New England, the Middle States, and the South. Racial heritage, religion, culture, and occupations could all be cited as reasons for a geographical split, and to some extent these factors did enter into the debates. Overriding them, however, was the fear that large states such as Virginia, Pennsylvania, and Massachusetts, with their greater wealth and much bigger populations, would dominate the weaker states in the union. As a result, small states such as Delaware, Connecticut, and New Jersey often found they had more in common with each other than with their larger and more powerful sectional neighbors. For this reason the delegates from the smaller states were generally less willing to grant the national government as much power as were those from the larger states.

On June 13 Nathaniel Gorham, chairman of the committee of the whole, presented a report that summarized Randolph's Virginia Plan, or at least those points on which there was now general agreement. The report contained nineteen resolutions and recommended that they be offered to the Congress, which in turn should submit them to the state legislatures. The legislatures might consider them directly or turn them over to specially created assemblies to decide on approval or rejection.

William Paterson of New Jersey then rose to call for

adjournment so that the report could be studied. The next morning he presented an alternative plan that contained the key demand of the small states: namely, that each state continue to have an equal voice in the Congress. The New Jersey Plan also provided for Congress to choose the executive, and it limited the authority of the national judiciary.

Defenders of the strong federal system were taken aback by the New Jersey Plan, for it differed in many ways from the Virginia Plan. Virginia's plan called for a two-house congress with representation based on population. New Jersey's plan called for a one-house congress in which each state would have an equal voice. The big-state (Virginia) plan guaranteed that a majority would prevail and that the legislature would have major lawmaking powers. It provided for an executive veto, authorized impeachment and removal procedures, an amending process, a multiple and powerful court system, a method for extension of national jurisdiction, and finally for ratification by all the people.

James Wilson of Virginia led the attack on the New Jersey Plan. The plan, he maintained, hardly increased congressional power, lacked a direct veto, allowed removal of the executive only by action of a majority of state governors, had no amending process, established a federal supreme court chosen by the executive authority, failed to set up a method for national territorial growth, and left the decision to ratify up to the state legislatures. In sum, the two plans illustrate the big- versus small-state conflict. The New Jersey Plan left the states equal in power to the proposed Congress. The Virginia Plan did not. It attempted to favor the states that had the most money and the largest population.

As the June 16 session ended, Randolph was eloquently defending the plan he had sponsored. The day being Saturday, delegates had until Monday morning to reexamine their thoughts on the issue. June 18, however, did not witness further discussion on the two plans. Instead, Alexander Hamilton took the floor to deliver the convention's second-longest speech. For five hours he expressed his own ideas about the best possible form that the new government might take. He proposed a new plan that he knew would be totally unacceptable to the other delegates. He praised the British system as "the only government in the world which unites public strength with individual security." His suggestions included a bicameral congress empowered to pass any laws whatsoever and a national governor elected for life and possessing an absolute veto. The ideas were an outrage to his audience. His purpose could hardly have been to change their minds. More likely Hamilton hoped his startling approach would make the propositions of the milder Federalists more acceptable to the advocates of state power.

On Tuesday the New Jersey Plan failed to gain approval, but the plan was resubmitted and the deadlock dragged on.

June 27 witnessed Luther Martin taking the floor to begin a rambling attack on the big states, which did not end until more than halfway through the next day. His speech marked one of the few times that a delegate questioned the sincerity of his opponent's motives. Old Benjamin Franklin was so disturbed by the growing bitterness that he rose to "implore the assistance of Heaven." He asked that future meetings be opened with a prayer. Hamilton and Williamson objected, and the proposal was voted down.

As July approached, the tension-building deadlock continued. A motion by Ellsworth of Connecticut on July 2 to allow each state a single vote in the second house of the legislature split the states five to five. Connecticut, New Jersey, Delaware, Maryland, and New York voted against Massachusetts, Pennsylvania, Virginia, and the Carolinas. Georgia divided evenly, and so could not vote. New Hampshire and Rhode Island were absent. In desperation, the convention grasped at a suggestion made by General Pinckney. It would adjourn for two days while a new "Grand Committee," including one man from each state, sought some expedient means of breaking the stalemate.

George Washington and Robert Morris spent their Fourth of July holiday trout fishing, while other delegates celebrated the nation's eleventh birthday by attending a benefit performance at the opera. Meanwhile, Gerry, Sherman, Yates, Paterson, Franklin, Bedford, Martin, Mason, Davie, Rutledge, and Baldwin prepared a fresh proposal for consideration on July 5. It proved more satisfactory to the small states than to the big ones. The first house (House of Representatives) would be apportioned according to population, with the suggestion that a ratio of one representative to 40,000 inhabitants be adopted. This house would also have the sole power to originate money bills. The second house (Senate), as the small states had never ceased to insist, granted each one an equal vote. In both houses, members would vote as individuals rather than as part of their state delegations.

Eleven more days were needed for argument and amendment before the final vote came. On July 16, by a vote of five to four, with Virginia, Pennsylvania, South Carolina, and Georgia in the negative and Massachusetts divided, the proposal of July 5, or the "Great Compromise" as it would henceforth be known, was adopted. Madison, King, and Wilson were particularly upset by the result, but the more moderate Federalists such as Gorham, Mason, Robert Morris, and Rutledge were satisfied. Credit for the remarkable achievement, sometimes called the Connecticut Plan, belonged primarily to Ellsworth, Sherman, and Johnson, the delegates from that state, who with the aid of Franklin and Dickinson had carried the day.

Even with the passage of the Great Compromise, other issues remained to be considered. For nine more working days the delegates struggled to make necessary decisions on the scope of congressional legislation, the jurisdiction of the national courts, and the length of terms of office. On the question of how the chief executive was to be chosen, sixty ballots were taken before James Wilson's idea of a presidential electoral system was molded into an acceptable form.

Finally, on July 26, the convention passed the net results of its labors to a committee on detail, then promptly adjourned for eleven days. Most of the exhausted delegates rested, and those living nearby returned to their homes. Meanwhile, the five-man committee on detail under the chairmanship of John Rutledge began the difficult task of organizing all the decisions of the past two months into some sort of logical and meaningful shape. The other members were Randolph, Wilson, Ellsworth, and Gorham, each from a different section of the country. With concentration and hard work they met the challenge. On Monday morning, August 6, each member of the reassembled convention received a folio pamphlet of seven pages with wide margins so that notes could be made. Only sixty copies, all closely guarded until the last possible moment, were printed by

Dunlap and Claypoole, who worked at night to meet the deadline. The document contained a preamble followed by twenty-three articles divided into forty-one sections.

Although the work of the committee on detail followed the direction given to it by the convention to organize those points already agreed upon, it did make a number of changes on its own. For example, the first and second houses of the national legislature were called the House of Representatives and the Senate. A far more important change was the listing of the specific powers to be granted to the Congress, which replaced the general statements of limitations that had been adopted up to this time.

By far the most explosive issue that now arose to plague the delegates was the question of slavery. Until now it had been almost completely ignored. All knew how dangerous an issue it might prove and that one day it must be faced. The time had come. Here indeed was a debate that divided the delegates along geographical lines, and it was one on which heated opinions and unbending stands would be taken.

The issue involved more than a decision as to the morality of slavery. A prime concern was whether slaves would be counted as part of the population when a census was conducted. Since slaves constituted 20 percent of the nation's inhabitants at the time, counting them would have greatly increased the number of southern seats in the House of Representatives. Control of the House would give the South great political power. On the other hand, if slaves were property rather than persons, the levying of direct taxes based on a head count would mean the South would pay less. Directly related was the problem of the slave trade itself. All the states except for the Carolinas and Georgia had already banned the importation of slaves, but these last three were firm in their claim that slave labor was necessary for their economic survival.

Rufus King attacked slavery, calling it "the curse of heaven." Gouverneur Morris joined in with a motion that would have awarded seats in the House of Representatives on the basis of one to 40,000 "free" inhabitants. The delegates rejected the addition of the word "free," but not before this dedicated hater of slavery declared, "I would sooner submit myself to a tax for paying for all the Negroes in the United States than saddle posterity with such a constitution."

The weary delegates, fearing the issue could destroy the convention, stopped the discussion without reaching a decision and quickly turned to other less controversial articles. Point by point every article was examined in detail and decisions were made. The term of a senator was set at six years, with one-third of them being elected every second year. The granting of a judicial veto power over legislation was rejected. The powers of the Congress were reworded and changed until the final result was a list of seventeen specific ones and the eighteenth, an "elastic clause," which gave Congress the right "to make all laws that shall be necessary and proper for carrying into execution the foregoing powers, and all other powers, vested by this constitution, in the government of the United States, or in any department or officer thereof."

The slave question flared up again in late August when Luther Martin attempted to tamper with a provision that banned interference with the slave trade. Again furious debate raged. George Mason, himself a slave owner, delivered the strongest attack on slavery that the delegates were to hear. Rutledge and the two Pinckneys fought back. An aroused Dickinson seconded Martin's efforts, and Ellsworth went so far as to call for the freeing of all the slaves already in the United States. As usual whenever no progress was being made, a new committee was created. Few were pleased with and some were ashamed of the results, but agreement was reached. Without ever using the words "slave" or "slavery," the Constitution would now provide that no interference with the importation of slaves could take place before 1808, except for the possibility of a ten-dollar tax on each arrival. Runaway or fugitive slaves were to be returned, even from free states, to their owners. Representatives and direct taxes apportioned among the states on the basis of population totals would include free inhabitants and "three-fifths of all other persons."

In exchange for these moderate restrictions on slavery, first, Congress was forbidden to tax exports—this protected southern earnings from trade with foreign countries. Second, a two-thirds vote was required in the Senate in order to ratify treaties—this guaranteed that one section would not be able to make business deals to its own advantage that would harm another region of the country.

The convention by now had lasted into September, far longer than anyone had imagined back in May. On Wednesday, the fifth day of the month, the legislature of Pennsylvania, which had generously given its home to the convention for the summer, was scheduled to reassemble. The delegates told their hosts that only a few more days would be needed to complete the task at hand. Graciously the state government took itself upstairs in the State House after assuring the visitors that they need not hurry.

Even without this added pressure, the end was in sight. Enough of the Constitution was now complete for delegates to say whether or not they would support the finished document. Luther Martin, who had once again lost his temper, left for Baltimore the day before, and was now busy writing an attack on what he called the errors and excesses of the convention. George Mason was still pleading that without a bill of rights the Constitution would be unacceptable, but he had little success in getting his fellow delegates to list the rights protected by the Constitution. Not a single state voted for his motion. Fearing for the future of the South under the new federal government, angry about its decisions concerning slavery, and shocked by the indifference toward the bill of rights he felt was so essential, Mason would now oppose adoption of the Constitution. So, too, would Elbridge Gerry, but since he had opposed almost everything that had happened during the past four months, this came as little surprise. Not so the decision of Edmund Randolph. The young and ambitious governor of Virginia, who had introduced the very plan out of which the Constitution had evolved, now had second thoughts. Afraid that the new government he had helped to construct was too revolutionary to win acceptance, he chose to remain neutral, saying that he would not sign the document or disclose what stand he would take when Virginia considered its ratification. Mason contemptuously called Randolph "Little Arnold" (after Benedict Arnold, the convicted traitor of the American Revolution) for the rest of his life.

Discussion now switched from the content of the Constitution to the method of its ratification. When completed and signed, the document would be sent to the Continental Congress, then sitting in New York City. From there, it was hoped, copies would be sent to the state legislatures with a request that they call individual ratifying conventions. When, and if, nine states agreed to accept the Constitution, it would go into effect. This was an illegal action under the terms of the Articles of Confederation, which stated that all amendments must be passed by unanimous consent. But then the Constitutional Convention itself was of doubtful legality, and in any case a vote of thirteen to zero was impossible. Rhode Island, which had refused to send a delegation to Philadelphia, could hardly be expected to accept the results of a convention whose very existence it had opposed.

On Saturday, September 8, the delegates established the last of their committees. William Samuel Johnson, Hamilton, Gouverneur Morris, King, and Madison were chosen as members of a committee on style. They struggled until the following Wednesday before completing a final polished draft. Gouverneur Morris did most of the writing and was the principal stylist of the Constitution; however, Judge Johnson acted as spokesman for the committee. With a new preamble, and the number of articles reduced from twenty-three to seven, the document was presented to the convention. Even now a few minor changes were made. George Washington proposed one. Speaking for the first time as a simple delegate, he requested and obtained unanimous consent to change the population ratio figure for the House of Representatives from 40,000 to 30,000.

A facsimile of the
first page of the
United States Constitution

We the People

of the United States, in order to form a more perfect Union, establish Justice, insure domestic Tranquility, provide for the common defence, promote the general Welfare, and secure the Blessings of Liberty to ourselves and our Posterity, do ordain and establish this Constitution for the United States of America.

Article. I.

Section. 1. All legislative Powers herein granted shall be vested in a Congress of the United States, which shall consist of a Senate and House of Representatives.

Section. 2. The House of Representatives shall be composed of Members chosen every second Year by the People of the several States, and the Electors in each State shall have the Qualifications requisite for Electors of the most numerous Branch of the State Legislature.

No Person shall be a Representative who shall not have attained to the Age of twenty five Years, and been seven Years a Citizen of the United States, and who shall not, when elected, be an Inhabitant of that State in which he shall be chosen.

Representatives and direct Taxes shall be apportioned among the several States which may be included within this Union, according to their respective Numbers, which shall be determined by adding to the whole Number of free Persons, including those bound to Service for a Term of Years, and excluding Indians not taxed, three fifths of all other Persons. The actual Enumeration shall be made within three Years after the first Meeting of the Congress of the United States, and within every subsequent Term of ten Years, in such Manner as they shall by Law direct. The Number of Representatives shall not exceed one for every thirty Thousand, but each State shall have at Least one Representative; and until such enumeration shall be made, the State of New Hampshire shall be entitled to chuse three, Massachusetts eight, Rhode Island and Providence Plantations one, Connecticut five, New York six, New Jersey four, Pennsylvania eight, Delaware one, Maryland six, Virginia ten, North Carolina five, South Carolina five, and Georgia three.

When vacancies happen in the Representation from any State, the Executive Authority thereof shall issue Writs of Election to fill such Vacancies.

The House of Representatives shall chuse their Speaker and other Officers; and shall have the sole Power of Impeachment.

Section. 3. The Senate of the United States shall be composed of two Senators from each State, chosen by the Legislature thereof, for six Years; and each Senator shall have one Vote.

Immediately after they shall be assembled in Consequence of the first Election, they shall be divided as equally as may be into three Classes. The Seats of the Senators of the first Class shall be vacated at the Expiration of the second Year, of the second Class at the Expiration of the fourth Year, and of the third Class at the Expiration of the sixth Year, so that one third may be chosen every second Year; and if Vacancies happen by Resignation, or otherwise, during the Recess of the Legislature of any State, the Executive thereof may make temporary Appointments until the next Meeting of the Legislature, which shall then fill such Vacancies.

No Person shall be a Senator who shall not have attained to the Age of thirty Years, and been nine Years a Citizen of the United States, and who shall not, when elected, be an Inhabitant of that State for which he shall be chosen.

The Vice President of the United States shall be President of the Senate, but shall have no Vote, unless they be equally divided.

The Senate shall chuse their other Officers, and also a President pro tempore, in the Absence of the Vice President, or when he shall exercise the Office of President of the United States.

The Senate shall have the sole Power to try all Impeachments. When sitting for that Purpose, they shall be on Oath or Affirmation. When the President of the United States is tried, the Chief Justice shall preside: And no Person shall be convicted without the Concurrence of two thirds of the Members present.

Judgment in Cases of Impeachment shall not extend further than to removal from Office, and disqualification to hold and enjoy any Office of honor, Trust or Profit under the United States: but the Party convicted shall nevertheless be liable and subject to Indictment, Trial, Judgment and Punishment, according to Law.

Section. 4. The Times, Places and Manner of holding Elections for Senators and Representatives, shall be prescribed in each State by the Legislature thereof; but the Congress may at any time by Law make or alter such Regulations, except as to the Places of chusing Senators.

The Congress shall assemble at least once in every Year, and such Meeting shall be on the first Monday in December, unless they shall by Law appoint a different Day.

Section. 5. Each House shall be the Judge of the Elections, Returns and Qualifications of its own Members, and a Majority of each shall constitute a Quorum to do Business; but a smaller Number may adjourn from day to day, and may be authorized to compel the Attendance of absent Members, in such Manner, and under such Penalties as each House may provide.

Each House may determine the Rules of its Proceedings, punish its Members for disorderly Behaviour, and, with the Concurrence of two thirds, expel a Member.

Each House shall keep a Journal of its Proceedings, and from time to time publish the same, excepting such Parts as may in their Judgment require Secrecy; and the Yeas and Nays of the Members of either House on any question shall, at the Desire of one fifth of those Present, be entered on the Journal.

Neither House, during the Session of Congress, shall, without the Consent of the other, adjourn for more than three days, nor to any other Place than that in which the two Houses shall be sitting.

Section. 6. The Senators and Representatives shall receive a Compensation for their Services, to be ascertained by Law, and paid out of the Treasury of the United States. They shall in all Cases, except Treason, Felony and Breach of the Peace, be privileged from Arrest during their Attendance at the Session of their respective Houses, and in going to and returning from the same; and for any Speech or Debate in either House, they shall not be questioned in any other Place.

No Senator or Representative shall, during the Time for which he was elected, be appointed to any civil Office under the Authority of the United States, which shall have been created, or the Emoluments whereof shall have been encreased during such time; and no Person holding any Office under the United States, shall be a Member of either House during his Continuance in Office.

Section. 7. All Bills for raising Revenue shall originate in the House of Representatives; but the Senate may propose or concur with Amendments as on other Bills.

Every Bill which shall have passed the House of Representatives and the Senate, shall, before it become a Law, be presented to the President of the

Then it was ordered that a copy of the Constitution be prepared for signing.

On Monday morning, September 17, the delegates gathered for the last time. It was a clear cool day, in delightful contrast to the long hot weeks of the past two months and the rainy weekend now ended. Of the fifty-five men who had participated in the deliberations, forty-one were present for the final ceremony. Ten supporters of the Constitution—Ellsworth, Strong, William Houstoun, Pierce, Martin, Davie, William Churchill Houston, McClurg, and Wythe—had already departed, along with John Dickinson, who was taken ill but left a letter with George Read authorizing him to sign his name. Four opponents —Lansing, Yates, Mercer, and Luther Martin—were also absent. After the Constitution was read, Benjamin Franklin asked for the floor. Too weak to deliver his own speech, it was read to the delegates by James Wilson. The message it contained was a plea for unity. Franklin confessed that like many others he had reservations about parts of the document, but ended by appealing that any man "who may still have objections to it, would with me, on this occasion, doubt a little of his own infallibility—and to make manifest our unanimity, put his name to this instrument."

To pacify further any doubtful signers, it was agreed to phrase the closing sentence "Done in convention, by the unanimous consent of the States present . . ." rather than requiring individual signatures committed to supporting the Constitution. In spite of all these efforts, however, Mason, Randolph, and Gerry still refused to sign. It was past three o'clock before the other thirty-eight delegates, ranging themselves according to the geography of the states from north to south, approached the dais to write the thirty-nine signatures that are found on the Constitution. Then, anxious to return the big square east room to the Pennsylvania legislators who were waiting patiently upstairs, the delegates adjourned the final session. Most of the delegates proceeded to the City Tavern on nearby Walnut Street for a farewell dinner. The next day they left for home. Although the Constitutional Convention of 1787 was over, the fight for ratification of the Constitution of the United States was just beginning.

The Ratification
Struggle

Although most of the delegates who had attended the Constitutional Convention were reasonably well pleased by what had been accomplished, all were gravely concerned about the reception, the people would give them when they returned home and the Constitution when its text was revealed. In spite of the crude communication and transportation systems of the day, their answer was not long in coming. The details of the Constitution became public knowledge in an amazingly short time. By September 19 the Philadelphia press had printed the complete text. The Continental Congress in New York City received its copy the very next day. By the end of October the document was being discussed across the land.

The supporters of the Constitution, Federalists, expected strong opposition from powerful anti-Federalists. Patrick Henry and Richard Henry Lee in Virginia; Lansing, Yates, and Governor George Clinton in New York; Luther Martin and Samuel Chase in Maryland; and Sam Adams and Elbridge Gerry in Massachusetts were in the anti-Federalist camp.

At first the Federalists were pleasantly surprised by early and easy victories. Ratification took place in Delaware by unanimous consent on December 7, 1787. In Pennsylvania anti-Federalists tried to prevent the legislature from calling a convention to consider ratification by staying away so that there would be no quorum for a vote. The result was a riotous scene with two members of the assembly being dragged from their rooming house to the state house, where they were forced to keep their seats until the meeting opened. On December 12 Pennsylvania ratified the Constitution by a vote of 46 to 23.

Six days later, on December 18, New Jersey ratified unanimously, and on January 2, 1788, Georgia did the same. Ellsworth and Sherman led the fight that won approval by Connecticut on January 9, by a 128 to 40 vote.

Next to make a decision was the key state of Massachusetts. The legislature had called for a ratifying convention to meet in Boston on January 9. When it did, the Federalists were dismayed to find that a majority of the 355 men present were in the opposition. Fortunately, many of them were open to discussion and could possibly change their minds. Some, such as John Hancock, had not yet decided which way they would vote. The Federalists went to work to rally popular support and win Hancock's vote. The well-known Bostonian was known to be vain and ambitious. The Federalists suggested that Virginia would probably reject the Constitution, which would eliminate George Washington as the first president under the new government. The position, they implied, would almost certainly go to Hancock if Massachusetts ratified. The plan worked; Hancock declared his support, and on February 6 the state convention ratified by a 187 to 168 margin.

In spite of the efforts of Luther Martin and a better organized team of anti-Federalists, Maryland became the seventh state to ratify on April 26, by a vote of 63 to 11. Then South Carolina made it eight on May 23, with a 149 to 73 decision.

In only nine months the Constitution had come within one state vote of victory, but now the odds shifted strongly to the side of the anti-Federalists. The Rhode Island state legislature refused to call a convention. Instead, on March 24, it held a popular referendum, which the Federalists boycotted, with the result that the Constitution was defeated 2,942 to 237.

Conditions in New Hampshire were not much more encouraging. In this northernmost of all the states, the anti-Federalists seemed to have won another victory. The convention that met at Exeter on February 13 had a majority of delegates opposed to the Constitution. As a result, the Federalists changed their strategy. Elsewhere they had always called for immediate action. Now they wanted the vote put off until later. They called for postponement. A week of frantic activity followed, at the end of which, by the narrow margin of five votes, the convention adjourned for several months. By the time it met again, the Federalists were in a stronger position. Other states had ratified, a bill of rights was promised, and so was an anti-slavery amendment. On June 14 New Hampshire ratified by a vote of 57 to 46.

The Federalists knew there was little hope a new government could succeed unless the large and powerful states accepted the Constitution. The struggle for ratification in Virginia, therefore, was important, for the state was the largest in the Union. There the Federalists faced the most brilliant and best-organized opponents. The anti-Federalists were led by Virginia's most respected leaders, Patrick Henry and George Mason, James Monroe, John Tyler—the father of a future president—Benjamin Harrison, and Richard Henry Lee.

The Federalists did not lack impressive leaders of their own. Judge Edmund Pendleton was the presiding officer. George Wythe, whose wife's illness had prevented him from spending more than a few days as a delegate to the Philadelphia convention, was now present and active. So were George Nicholas, the only man rated as fine an orator as Patrick Henry; John Marshall; and, of course, James Madison.

The Constitution was examined clause by clause, and again, as in the cases of Massachusetts, Maryland, and New Hampshire, amendments were suggested. Clearly the men at Philadelphia would have done well had they listened to George Mason's call for a bill of rights. The absence of such guarantees was proving to be the greatest fault in the Constitution. The Federalist cause was much strengthened when Edmund Randolph gave his support to the Constitution, adding that the necessary amendments could be added after ratification. The anti-Federalists doubted that such a pledge would be guaranteed; still, on June 25 the Constitution succeeded by 89 to 79.

The last of the big states, New York, witnessed an incredible struggle. Ratification was opposed by Lansing, Yates, and Melancton Smith, but now supported by the state's most important political figure, Governor George Clinton. The Federalist champion was Alexander Hamilton, who, in spite of his disappointment at what he considered to be severe shortcomings in the Constitution, worked to the point of exhaustion for its ratification.

Out of the struggle came eighty-five essays published in the press. They would come to be known as the Federalist Papers, perhaps the most brilliant and original work in the field of government ever written in the United States. Hamilton wrote fifty-one of them, Madison contributed twenty-nine, and New York's other leading Federalist, John Jay, added five.

When the convention met at Poughkeepsie on June 17, the anti-Federalists were in the majority. Clinton, somewhat taken aback by Virginia's decision, offered to delay if Hamilton would agree to an attempt to add amendments prior to a vote by calling the Constitutional Convention back for a second session in Philadelphia. Realizing that this was an attempt to reopen the document for a host of changes from other states as well as New York, Hamilton gambled and called for an immediate vote. By the narrowest of margins, 30 to 27, the motion to ratify carried. A long list of thirty-two suggested amendments was recommended.

Ratification by New York meant that eleven of the thirteen states had approved the new Constitution. It had been rejected by North Carolina and Rhode Island. Over a year later North Carolina reversed its decision by a 194 to 77 margin. Rhode Island, under threat of economic boycott (the Senate actually voted to stop business relations between the U.S. government and the state) finally approved the Constitution by a 34 to 32 vote on May 29, 1790.

The Constitutional Convention had lasted for four months. It had presented an extraordinary blueprint for a new federal union to a people who jealously guarded the freedom they had seized only eleven years before. With grave doubts and a considerable hesitation that lasted up to two years, they agreed to give up some of those powers to the new government under the Constitution.

The document has proved flexible enough to meet the demands of an industrial society that did not exist at the time it was written. Allowing for an army and navy, it has met the challenge of the airplane, the submarine, and the nuclear bomb. Under its flag the nation has grown in size and population. Depressions, assassinations, and corruption have tested its strength, but it has yet to fail. Nations born since 1787 have patterned their own governments after that of the United States, but none with as much success. If one can discount the first ten amendments—the Bill of Rights—which were added less than two years after the last of the states ratified the Constitution, it is a striking fact that the American people have felt it necessary to make only sixteen changes in the two-centuries-old instrument of government.

The Constitution has survived invasion by foreign enemies, one of the bloodiest civil wars in history, two world wars, and all the problems associated with being the basis of law in the most powerful nation in the world—the United States of America.

Bibliography

The following works have been helpful in the writing of this book and will be of assistance to any reader who wishes to probe more deeply into the subject.

Bowen, Catherine Drinker. *Miracle at Philadelphia: The Story of the Constitutional Convention May to September 1787*. Boston: Little, Brown, 1966.

Broderick, Francis L. *The Origins of the Constitution 1776–1789*. New York: Macmillan, 1964.

Chidsey, Donald Barr. *The Birth of the Constitution: An Informal History*. New York: Crown Publishers, 1964.

Cooke, Donald E. *America's Great Document—the Constitution*. New York: Hammond Incorporated, 1970.

Donovan, Frank Robert. *Mr. Madison's Constitution: The Story behind the Constitutional Convention*. New York: Dodd Mead, 1965.

Jensen, Merrill. *The Making of the American Constitution*. Princeton, N.J.: Van Nostrand, 1964.

McDonald, Forrest and Ellen S., eds. *Confederation and Constitution 1781–1789*. New York: Harper and Row, 1968.

Mitchell, Broadus and Louise. *A Biography of the Constitution of the United States: Its Origin, Formation, Adoption, Interpretation*. New York: Oxford University Press, 1964.

Rossiter, Clinton Lawrence. *1787: The Grand Convention*. New York: Macmillan, 1966.

Smith, David G. *The Convention and the Constitution*. New York: St. Martin's Press, 1965.

Van Doren, Carl. *The Great Rehearsal: The Story of the making and ratifying of the Constitution of the United States*. New York: Viking Press, 1948.

Wilson, Fred Taylor. *Our Constitution and Its Makers*. New York: Fleming H. Revell, 1937.

Index

Adams, John, 5, 7, 46
Adams, Samuel, 46, 74
Albany Plan of Union, 11
Allen, Ethan, 7
Anglican Church, 15
Army, Continental, 7, 13, 14
Arnold, Benedict, 7
Articles of Confederation, 1, 10–14

Baldwin, Abraham, 3, 49, 64
Bassett, Richard, 2, 36
Bedford, Gunning, Jr., 2, 36, 46, 64
Bill of Rights, 69, 76, 77, 79
Blair, John, 3, 32
Blount, William, 3, 39
Boston Tea Party, 4
Brearly, David, 2, 41, 44
Broom, Jacob, 2, 36
Bunker Hill, Battle of, 7
Butler, Pierce, 3, 40–41, 53

Canada, 7, 16
Carroll, Daniel, 3, 50
Catholics, 52
Chase, Samuel, 74
China, 20
Clark, Abraham, 41
Clinton, George, 35, 74, 77
Clymer, George, 2, 30
Coercive Acts, 4–5
Congress, Continental, 7–14

Congress of the Confederation, 16–23
    delegates, 1
Connecticut, 6, 11, 30, 58, 61, 64
    delegates, 1
    ratification, 75
Connecticut Plan, 65
Constitution, U.S.
    ratification, 69
    signers, 1–3
Constitutional Convention
    delegates, 1–3, 25–28
Continental Army, 7
Continental Association, 5
Continental Congress, 7–14
    First, 1–3, 4
    Second, 1–3, 6, 7–11
Currency, 19

Dana, Francis, 45
Davie, William Richardson, 3, 38, 64, 72
Dayton, Jonathan, 2, 26, 40, 41–44
Debts, 18, 21
Declaration of Independence, 1, 9
Declaration of Rights, 5
Delaware, 24, 30, 36, 58, 61, 64
    delegates, 2
    ratification, 74
Dickinson, John, 2, 7, 9, 10, 13, 25, 36–37, 65, 68, 72

Ellsworth, Oliver, 1, 46–48, 64, 65, 68, 72, 75
Executive office, 59–60, 62, 65
Exports, 5

Federalism, 30, 31, 32, 36, 57, 63, 74, 76, 77
Federalist Papers, 77
Few, William, 3, 44, 49
First Continental Congress, 4
    delegates, 1
Fitzsimons, Thomas, 2, 31
France, 10, 20
Franklin, Benjamin, 2, 10, 11, 13, 25, 26, 30, 52, 57, 59, 63, 64, 65, 72

Gage, Thomas, 7
Galloway, Joseph, 4
George III, king of England, 4, 6
Georgia, 30, 67
    delegates, 3
    ratification, 75
Gerry, Elbridge, 1, 45, 46, 58, 60, 64, 69, 72, 74
Gilman, Nicholas, 1, 51
Gorham, Nathaniel, 1, 45, 54, 61, 65
Government, colonial, 11–15
Great Britain, 4, 6
    trade with Indians, 18
Great Compromise, 65

Hamilton, Alexander, 2, 24, 35, 52, 58, 60, 63, 70, 77, 79

Hancock, John, 45, 46, 75
Harrison, Benjamin, 76
Henry, Patrick, 32, 74, 76
House of Representatives, 64, 66–68, 70
Houston, William Churchill, 2, 41, 72
Houstoun, William, 3, 49, 72
Huntington, Samuel, 11
Hutchinson, Thomas, 11

Imports, 5
Indians, 18
Ingersoll, Jared, 2, 31
Intolerable Acts, 4–5

Jackson, William, 29
Jay, John, 77
Jefferson, Thomas, 5, 7, 9, 19, 25
Jenifer, Daniel of St. Thomas, 2, 5
Johnson, William Samuel, 1, 48, 65, 70
Judiciary, national, 60

King, Rufus, 1, 44–45, 67, 70

Land disputes, 10–11, 15, 16–18
Langdon, John, 1, 51
Lansing, John, Jr., 2, 35, 36, 72, 74, 77
Lee, Richard Henry, 9, 74, 76
Legislature, national, 55–58, 60, 64–66
Livingston, William, 2, 41, 60

McClurg, James, 3, 32, 72
McHenry, James, 2, 46, 50
Madison, James, Jr., 3, 24, 28–29, 30, 31, 32, 59, 70, 77
Marshall, John, 77
Martin, Alexander, 3, 38
Martin, Luther, 3, 50–51, 63, 64, 67, 68, 69, 72, 74, 75
Maryland, 10–11, 16, 24, 30, 64, 77
  delegates, 2–3
  ratification, 75
Mason, George, 3, 32, 33–35, 58, 64, 67, 69, 72, 76, 77
Massachusetts, 4, 5, 6, 11, 21, 30, 44, 46, 58, 59, 61, 64, 77
  delegates, 1
  ratification, 75
Mercer, John Francis, 3, 50, 72
Mifflin, Thomas, 2, 31
Monroe, James, 76
Morris, Gouverneur, 2, 29, 31, 58, 67, 70
Morris, Robert, 2, 19, 25, 31, 52

Navy, 7, 13, 14
Netherlands, 20
New England Restraining Act, 6
New Hampshire, 6, 16, 30, 64, 77
  delegates, 1
  ratification, 76
New Jersey, 20, 24, 30, 41, 58, 61, 64
  delegates, 2
  ratification, 75

New Jersey Plan, 62–63
New Orleans, 18
New York, 6, 11, 16, 20, 24, 30, 35, 36, 58, 64
  delegates, 2
  ratification, 77–78
Nicholas, George, 76–77
Nielson, John, 41
North, Lord, 5
North Carolina, 30, 37–38, 58, 64, 66–67
  delegates, 3
  ratification, 78
Northwest Territory, 20

Parliament, British, 4–6
Paterson, William, 2, 41, 44, 61–62, 64
Pendleton, Edmund, 76
Pennsylvania, 16, 24, 29, 30–31, 58, 61, 64
  delegates, 2
  ratification, 74–75
Philadelphia, 4, 29
Pierce, William, 3, 49–50, 72
Pinckney, Charles, 3, 39–40, 52, 59, 68
Pinckney, Charles Cotesworth, 3, 26, 39–40, 64, 68
Potomac River, 24

Randolph, Edmund Jennings, 3, 28, 32, 33, 53, 57, 59, 63, 65, 69, 72, 77

Read, George, 2, 36, 37, 60, 72

Religion, 52

Rhode Island, 19, 25, 64, 70, 75–76
    ratification, 78

Rutledge, John, 3, 39, 52, 59, 64, 65, 67

Second Continental Congress, 6, 7–11
    delegates, 1

Senate, U.S., 64, 66–68

Shays' Rebellion, 21–23

Sherman, Roger, 1, 48–49, 57, 58, 64, 65, 75

Slavery, 14, 66–68

Smith, Melancton, 77

South Carolina, 18, 30, 39, 58, 64, 66–67
    delegates, 3
    ratification, 75

Spaight, Richard Dobbs, 3, 38, 53

Spain, 18–19

State government, 60–62

Strong, Caleb, 1, 45, 72

Suffolk Resolves, 5

Suffrage, 57

Sullivan, John, 51

Sweden, 20

Tariffs, 20

Taxation, 5, 13, 20, 68

Tennessee, 16

Territories, 10–11, 20, 62

Trade, 5–6, 15, 18–19, 20

Tyler, John, 76

Vermont, 16

Virginia, 4, 11, 30, 32, 33, 58, 61, 64
    delegates, 3
    ratification, 76–77

Virginia Plan, 53–63

Warren, Joseph, 5

Washington, George, 3, 7, 25, 26, 28, 29, 32, 52, 54, 70, 75

Williamson, Hugh, 3, 38, 63

Wilson, James, 2, 29, 31, 58, 59, 62, 65, 72

Wythe, George, 3, 32, 52, 72, 76

Yates, Robert, 2, 35, 36, 58, 64, 72, 74, 77

About the Author

The Constitutional Convention is a familiar subject to Harold Cecil Vaughan. A student and teacher of history over the past twenty-five years, he has been on the faculty of the Collegiate School in New York City and the Brooklyn Friends School and now teaches at Ridgewood High School in New Jersey. A native New Yorker, he served in the Army Air Corps after receiving his A.B. degree from Columbia College, and returned to Columbia University for his M.A. and further graduate study. He is an avid fan of the legitimate theater and his alma mater's football team. Mr. Vaughan has also lectured on historical subjects to the National Society of the Colonial Dames in New York and has been a guest speaker to the Junior League, the Long Island Historical Association, and the Contemporary Club. His previous books for Franklin Watts include *The Citizen Genet Affair*, *The Hayes-Tilden Election of 1876*, *The XYZ Affair*, and *The Monroe Doctrine* (all Focus Books), and *The Versailles Treaty* (a World Focus Book).